THE ULTIMATE FOOTBALL ACTIVITY BOOK

THE ULTIMATE FOOTBALL ACTIVITY BOOK

Football Jokes by Sandy Ransford
Illustrated by Alan Rowe

Football Puzzles by Sandy Ransford
Illustrated by David Mostyn

Football Crosswords by
Roy and Sue Preston

MACMILLAN CHILDREN'S BOOKS

Football Jokes and *Football Puzzles* first published 1998
He Shoots He Scores (Football Crosswords) first published 1995

This edition published 2006 by Macmillan Children's Books
a division of Macmillan Publishers Limited
20 New Wharf Road, London N1 9RR
Basingstoke and Oxford
Associated companies throughout the world
www.panmacmillan.com

ISBN 978-0-330-44275-6

Football Jokes and *Football Puzzles*: text copyright © Sandy Ransford 1998
Football Crosswords: puzzles copyright © Roy and Sue Preston 1995
Football Jokes: illustrations copyright © Alan Rowe 1998
Football Puzzles: illustrations copyright © David Mostyn 1998

5 7 9 8 6

A CIP catalogue record for this book is available from
the British Library.

Typeset by Nigel Hazle
Printed and bound in Great Britain by CPI Mackays, Chatham ME5 8TD

Football Jokes
1

Football Puzzles
97

Football Crosswords
193

FOOTBALL JOKES

by Sandy Ransford
Illustrated by Alan Rowe

For Daniel, Robert, Tommy and William

Contents

Kick-Off

Why do people play football?
For kicks.

What can light up a dull evening?
A football match.

Young Alec came off the pitch looking very dejected, and slunk into the dressing room. 'I've never played so badly before,' he sighed.

'Oh,' answered a fellow player. 'You've played before, have you?'

TEACHER: What form are you in, lad?
BILLY: Well, I scored two goals last Saturday.

DAD: How did this window get broken?
TOMMY: Er, my football took a shot at goal while I was cleaning it.

A football fan was driving the wrong way down a one-way street when he was stopped by a policeman, who asked where he was going. 'To the match,' he answered. 'But I must be too late – everyone else is coming back.'

TEACHER: And why were you late for school today, Jimmy?
JIMMY: *I was dreaming about a football match and they went into extra time.*

A tourist visiting London stopped a man carrying a football and asked, 'How do I get to Wembley?'
   'Practice,' was the reply.

How can you stop moles digging up the football pitch?
Hide their spades.

MOTHER MONSTER: Why don't you go out and play football with your little brother?
LITTLE MONSTER: *Oh Mum, I'd much rather play with a real football.*

Why was the mummy no good at football?
He was too wrapped up in himself.

What's the best thing to do when a soccer ball is in the air?
Use your head.

What did the pitch say to the player?
'I hate it when people treat me like dirt.'

What's the difference between the Prince of Wales and a throw-in?
One's heir to the throne; the other's thrown in the air.

YOUNG FAN: Did you say you learned to play football in six easy lessons?
STAR PLAYER: Yes. It was the 600 that came afterwards that were difficult!

BRITISH PLAYER: Where were you born?
FOREIGN PLAYER: In Italy.
BRITISH PLAYER: Which part?
FOREIGN PLAYER: All of me, of course!

Which international player has the biggest head?
The one with the biggest hat.

FIRST FAN: Are you superstitious?
SECOND FAN: No.
FIRST FAN: Good. Then lend me £13 to get into the match.

What's Ryan Giggs's favourite supper?
Fish and chipping.

What language would two Ruud Gullits speak?
Double Dutch.

What happened when the boy footballer married a girl footballer?
People said it was a perfect match.

When is a footballer like a baby?
When he dribbles.

When is a footballer like a grandfather clock?
When he's a striker.

When is a kick like a boat?
When it's a punt.

MATHS TEACHER: Who can explain to me what net profit is?
SMART SAMMY: When your team wins 6–0.

A football fan went to an away match and stopped for a drink at a pub on his way home. As he was leaving he saw someone had painted his car in the opposing team's colours. Very angry, he went back into the pub and demanded loudly, 'All right, right, then, who painted my car?'

A very large man with a broken nose and a large stick in his hand slowly got to his feet.

'I did,' he said. 'What about it?'

'Er, I just wanted you to know it's a great improvement,' stammered the fan.

When can a footballer move as fast as a Porche?
When he's inside it.

YOUNG BRYAN: Were you any good at football, Dad?

DAD: Well, I once ran down the pitch faster than any other player. And if I ever find out who put that wasp in my shorts, I'll murder him!

How do you stop a hot and sweaty footballer from smelling?

Put a peg on his nose!

What's large and grey and carries a trunk and two pairs of football boots?

An elephant who's just joined the team.

Why did Rovers win 12–0?

They had an elephant in goal.

What do you do if you're too hot at a football match?

Sit next to a fan.

What did the ball say to the footballer?

'I get a kick out of you.'

JIM: How should I have kicked that ball?

TIM: Under an assumed name.

HARRY: Every night I dream about football – of running down the pitch, passing the ball, avoiding tackles . . .
LARRY: Don't you ever dream about girls?
HARRY: What? And miss a chance at goal?

Why are there fouls in football?
Same reason there are ducks in cricket.

YOUNG FOOTBALLER: How do I stand for a test trial?
SELECTOR: You don't stand, you grovel.

It was a boring and disappointing match, with very little action.

'I'm surprised the spectators don't yell at them,' said a man in the stand.

'Difficult to shout while you're asleep,' replied his friend.

KEN: I've just been to the doctor and he said I can't play football.
BEN: Oh? When did he see you play?

11

MR BLACK: Why are you so sad?
MR WHITE: My wife ran off with my best friend yesterday.
MR BLACK: Oh dear.
MR WHITE: Yes, and it means we'll have no centre forward tomorrow.

Why can't horses play football?
Because they've got two left feet.

Which fish is a famous footballer?
Finny Jones.

Which footballer sailed down the field like a yacht?
Gary Spinnaker.

The doctor was giving members of the team a medical. 'Breathe out three times,' he said to one of the players.

'Are you checking my lungs?' asked the player.

'No, I'm going to clean my spectacles,' replied the doctor.

How can a footballer stop his nose running?
Put out a foot and trip it up.

BRIAN: I love playing football. I could play like this for ever.
RYAN: Don't you ever want to get any better?

A black-and-white cat walked across the pitch in front of the team two weeks ago.
Since then our luck has been very patchy.

How does an octopus go on to a football pitch?
Well armed!

Why was the centipede no use to the football team?
He never arrived on the pitch until half-time – it took him that long to lace up his boots.

Which animal plays football sitting cross-legged?
Yoga Bear.

What two things should a footballer never eat before breakfast?
Lunch and dinner.

Why is football like fresh milk?
It strengthens the calves.

What's black and white and wears dark glasses?
A football in disguise.

Two flies were playing football in a saucer. One said to the other, 'We'll have to do better than this: we're playing in the cup next week!'

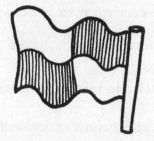

Two football fans were up in court for fighting. One fan had bitten off part of the other's ear, and the judge told him he was fined £200.

'But it was self-defence,' he protested.

The judged ignored him. 'Fined £200 and bound over to keep the peace for a year,' he pronounced.

'I can't do that,' said the fan. 'I threw it in a dustbin.'

What happened when a herd of cows had a football match?
There was udder chaos.

What's the difference between a flea-ridden dog and a bored football spectator?
One's going to itch; the other's itching to go.

What can a footballer never make right?
His left foot.

POLICE SERGEANT: No trouble with football fans
this week, constable.
POLICE CONSTABLE: No, sir. Why was that?
POLICE SERGEANT: United were playing away.

How do ghost footballers keep fit?
With regular exorcise.

SPORTS JOURNALIST: Tell me more gossip about the
goings-on at Rovers.
***ROVERS PLAYER: I can't. I've already told you
more than I heard myself.***

How do you hire a professional footballer?
Stand him on a chair.

What has two feet like a footballer, two eyes like a
footballer and two arms like a footballer, yet isn't a
footballer?
A photograph of a footballer.

Alan and Brian sat down to watch a video of the 1997 Cup Final. Alan bet Brian £20 that Chelsea would win.

'OK,' said Brian. 'You're on.'

Chelsea did win, but Alan confessed he couldn't take Brian's money, as he'd already heard the results before watching the video.

'So had I,' said Brian. 'But I didn't think Middlesbrough would lose a second time.'

Darren and Sharon were playing football one evening, trying to kick the ball into a 'goal' marked out on a wall.

'We'd better go, it's getting dark,' said Darren. 'And we haven't scored a single goal yet.'

'Let's miss a few more before we go,' said Sharon.

Team Spirit

Which football team never meets before a match?
Queen's Park Strangers.

Which football team should you not eat in a sandwich?
Oldham.

In a theatre a magician was introducing his act. 'I will show you the mysteries of the Orient,' he said.

A voice from the audience called out, 'But what about Millwall? They could do with a bit of magic as well!'

MIKE: Did you hear that the local team now plays the National Anthem before each match?
SPIKE: Are they that patriotic?
MIKE: No. They play it to make sure everyone in the team can stand up.

LENNY: The Leeds manager said I'd make a great footballer if it weren't for two things.
BENNY: What were they?
LENNY: My feet.

'Our team's doing so badly that if they win a corner they do a lap of honour.'

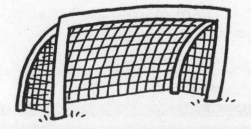

What do you call the person in the team who carries a broom?

The sweeper.

MR GREEN: I've been invited to join the firm's football team. They want me to play for them very badly.

MR BROWN: In that case, you're just the man.

Manchester United were playing Chelsea at Stamford Bridge. A man wearing a bright red-and-white rosette walked up to the ticket office and asked the price of admission.

'£50, sir,' said the attendant.

'Here's £25,' replied the man. 'There's only one team worth watching.'

Jack was a keen Torquay supporter. 'All Torquay have to do to get out of Division Two is to win eight of their next three matches,' he said.

FOOTBALLER: I've had an idea which might help the team win a few matches.

CAPTAIN: Good. When are you emigrating?

SCOTTISH TEAM CAPTAIN: How can we raise the level of our game?

SCOTTISH TEAM MANAGER: Play at the top of Ben Nevis?

Which is the best US city for a visit by a football team that likes dancing?

San Frandisco.

What's yellow, has 22 legs and peels off at half time?
Banana United.

After the match the team was in the dressing room when the trainer came in and asked if anyone had seen his spectacles.

'Yes,' replied one of the players. 'They were out on the pitch.'

'Then why didn't you bring them in?' asked the trainer.

'I didn't think you'd want them after everyone had trodden on them,' replied the player.

Why did the dumbo in the team climb on to the café roof at the celebration dinner?
He'd heard the meal was on the house.

The architect was showing the team round the new stadium. 'I think you'll find it's flawless,' he said proudly.

'What do we walk on then?' asked one of the players.

FIRST PLAYER: Wasn't the captain angry when you said you were leaving the team next month?
SECOND PLAYER: Yes. He thought it was this month.

Which member of the team flies down the field?
The winger.

Which member of the team can always keep fit,
providing he has a short length of rope?
The skipper.

The school football team was going to France to play
a team in their twin town.

On board the ferry, the head teacher was giving
them instructions. 'Now what would you do if a boy
falls overboard?' he asked.

'Shout "boy overboard",' called out one of the
players.

'Good,' said the teacher. 'And what would you do
if a teacher falls overboard?'

'Er, which one, sir?' asked another player
nervously.

Which football team can you find in *Whooo's Whooo?*
The Owls.

Why did the potato go to the match?
So it could root for the home team.

Why is a scrambled egg like Manchester United in the
2005 FA Cup Final?
Because they're both beaten.

What happened to the snowman who left the football team?
He just drifted around.

What position did the ducks play in the soccer team?
Right and left quack.

Which football team comes out of an ice-cream van?
Aston Vanilla.

Which football team spends all its spare time at pop concerts?
Blackburn Ravers.

What was the star player awarded when he missed a penalty?
A constellation prize.

MILLY: Did you hear the football club was burgled – but all they took were the soap and towels from the players' dressing room?
WILLY: The dirty crooks.

At the annual dinner and dance of the local football club the band was so awful that when someone sounded the fire alarm everyone got up to dance.

A man was up in court, charged with trying to set fire to Chelsea's grandstand.

When questioned by the judge he said he had a burning interest in football.

MRS ROUND: I hear your son has a place in the school football team. What position does he play?
MRS LONG: I think he's one of the drawbacks.

A man went to meet the members of a vegetable soccer team.

'This stick of celery is our goalie; the carrots are our centre forwards; and the onions are our backs,' explained his host.

'And what's that one over there, telling everyone else what to do?' the man asked, pointing to a mud-covered vegetable that was lounging around.

'Oh him?' replied the host. 'He's our coach potato.'

Why do Moscow Dynamo play such a fast game?
Because they're always rushin'.

What team is good in an omelette?
Best Ham.

What was the monkey in the team specially good at?
Banana shots.

'Stop the ball! Stop the ball!' the PE teacher yelled to the inexperienced goalie. 'Why didn't you?'

'I thought that was what the net was for,' *sniffed the poor boy.*

A Sheffield man was asked why his car was painted red on one side and blue on the other. 'Because I can't decide whether to support United or Wednesday,' he explained.

FIRST PLAYER: Why do you call the team captain Camera?
SECOND PLAYER: Because he's always snapping at me.

If it takes 20 men six months to build a grandstand at the football pitch, how long would it take 40 men to build it?
No time at all, because the 20 men had already completed it!

ANDY: That new chap is a wonder player.
SANDY: Why do you call him that?
ANDY: Because I look at him and wonder if he's ever played before!

DON: How's the new player coming along?
RON: He's trying.
DON: I've heard he's very trying.

When Harry retired from the team he said he was going to work in a bank.

'Why do you want to do that?' asked Larry.

'I've heard there's money in it,' replied Harry.

The club advertised for a handyman, and Mr Perkins came for an interview.

'Well, Mr Perkins,' said the manager, 'what qualifications do you have for this job? Are you handy?'

'I reckon so,' replied Mr Perkins. 'I only live next door.'

MANAGER: This dressing room is disgusting! It hasn't been cleaned for a month!
CLEANER: Don't blame me. I've only been here for a fortnight.

'United's such a poor team there's always a long queue at their ground – trying to get out!'

Why did the elephant paint his toenails red?
So he could hide in a pile of Manchester United shirts.

Why did the elephant wear a red-and-white shirt?
So he could play for Manchester United.

Weedy Willie was rather underweight and was told by his doctor that he'd be a better footballer if he put on a few pounds. 'Tell you what, said the doctor, 'eat a plum. If you swallow it whole you'll gain a stone.'

What do you call a noisy soccer fan?
A foot-bawler.

Why did the manager have the pitch flooded?
He wanted to bring on his sub.

The leading striker kept looking at the grandstand.
    'Are you thinking of kicking the ball up there?' asked another player.
    'My mother-in-law's sitting there,' explained the striker.
    'But even you will never hit her from here,' replied his team mate.

What happened when the footballer went to see his doctor complaining about flat feet?
The doctor gave him a bicycle pump.

'Football, football,' sighed Mrs Jones. 'That's all you think of. I bet you don't even remember when we got married.'

'I certainly do,' said Mr Jones. 'It was the day Arsenal beat West Ham 6–0.'

My mum says she'll leave my dad if he doesn't stop watching football.'

'Oh dear. That's awful.'

'Yes. Dad says he'll really miss her.'

PE TEACHER: Andy, you're hopeless at football, cricket and tennis. I don't think you'll ever be first at anything.

ANDY: I'm always first in the dinner queue, sir.

How many people can you fit into an empty football stadium?
Only one. After that it isn't empty any more.

GERTIE: I'm so pleased you're going to mow the lawn for Dad this afternoon.

BERTIE: Why?

GERTIE: Because then I can borrow your football.

What goes in pink and comes out blue?
A footballer who plays for a team that only has cold showers.

KELLY: While Darren was taking a shower after the match, someone stole all his clothes.
NELLIE: Oh dear! What did he come home in?
KELLY: The dark!

TALENT SCOUT: Your number six looks as if he might be a good footballer if his legs weren't so short.
TEAM MANAGER: They're not that short. They do both reach the floor.

Why did the footballer put his bed in the fireplace?
He wanted to sleep like a log.

Knock, knock.
Who's there?
Aladdin.
Aladdin who?
Aladdin the street's waiting for you to
come out and play football.

Knock, knock.
Who's there?
Accordion.
Accordion who?
Accordion to the paper United will win today.

Knock, knock.
Who's there?
Alison.
Alison who?
Alison to the football results on the
radio.

Knock, knock.
Who's there?
Euripides.
Euripides who?
Euripides football shorts and you buy me a new pair!

Knock, knock.
Who's there?
Godfrey.
Godfrey who?
Godfrey tickets for the match on
Saturday.

Knock, knock.
Who's there?
Juno.
Juno who?
Juno what time the kick-off is?

Knock, knock.
Who's there?
Kerry.
Kerry who?
Kerry me off the pitch, I think my leg's
broken.

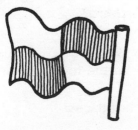

Knock, knock.
Who's there?
Ooze.
Ooze who?
Ooze free kick was that?

Knock, knock.
Who's there?
Al B.
Al B who?
Al B home straight after the match.

Knock, knock.
Who's there?
Felix.
Felix who?
Felixcited about going to the Cup Tie.

Knock, knock.
Who's there?
Java.
Java who?
Java spare pair of bootlaces?

Knock, knock.
Who's there?
Howell.
Howell who?
Howell you take that corner.

Knock, knock.
Who's there?
Kipper.
Kipper who?
Kipper your hands off the ball!

Knock, knock.
Who's there?
Ammonia.
Ammonia who?
Ammonia little boy and I can't run as fast as you.

Knock, knock.
Who's there?
Weed.
Weed who?
Weed like to win this game.

Knock, knock.
Who's there?
Ida.
Ida who?
Ida terrible time getting to the match – all the buses
were full.

Knock, knock.
Who's there?
Howard.
Howard who?
Howard the ground is when you dive for
a save!

Knock, knock.
Who's there?
Money.
Money who?
Money hurts since I twisted it on the pitch.

Knock, knock.
Who's there?
Venice.
Venice who?
Venice the next away match?

Knock, knock.
Who's there?
Francis.
Francis who?
Francis where Thierry Henry comes from.

Knock, knock.
Who's there?
Stu.
Stu who?
Stu late to score a goal now.

Knock, knock.
Who's there?
Harvey.
Harvey who?
Harvey going to have another game before lunch?

Knock, knock.
Who's there?
Waiter.
Waiter who?
Waiter minute while I tie my bootlaces.

Knock, knock.
Who's there?
Yale.
Yale who?
Yale never win if you don't play your best.

Knock, knock.
Who's there?
Luke.
Luke who?
Luke, he's just scored a goal.

> Knock, knock.
> **Who's there?**
> Saul.
> **Saul who?**
> Saul over when the final whistle blows.

Knock, knock.
Who's there?
Oily.
Oily who?
Oily in the morning's the best time to train.

> Knock, knock.
> **Who's there?**
> Uriah.
> **Uriah who?**
> Keep Uriah on the ball.

Knock, knock.
Who's there?
Argo.
Argo who?
Argo to Elland Road on Saturdays.

Knock, knock.
Who's there?
General Lee.
General Lee who?
General Lee I support Chelsea but today
    I'm rooting for Fulham.

Knock, knock.
Who's there?
Alec.
Alec who?
Alec soccer but I don't like rugby.

Knock, knock.
Who's there?
Wooden.
Wooden who?
Wooden it be great if we won the cup?

Knock, knock.
Who's there?
Farmer.
Farmer who?
Farmer birthday I got a new pair of football boots.

Knock, knock.
Who's there?
Nana.
Nana who?
Nana your business who we put in goal.

Knock, knock.
Who's there?
Deceit.
Deceit who?
Deceit of your shorts is all muddy.

Knock, knock.
Who's there?
Hurd.
Hurd who?
Hurd my foot so I couldn't play today.

Knock, knock.
Who's there?
Ken.
Ken who?
Ken Harry come out and play football?

Knock, knock.
Who's there?
Stepfather.
Stepfather who?
One stepfather and you'll be over the touchline.

Knock, knock.
Who's there?
Police.
Police who?
Police let me play with your new football.

Knock, knock.
Who's there?
Scold.
Scold who?
Scold wearing shorts to play football in winter.

Knock, knock.
Who's there?
Ammon.
Ammon who?
Ammon awfully good football player – can I be in your team?

Knock, knock.
Who's there?
Omar.
Omar who?
Omar goodness, what a shot!

Knock, knock.
Who's there?
Les.
Les who?
Les go out and play football.

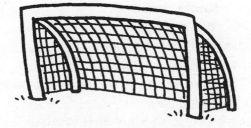

Knock, knock.
Who's there?
Lief Eric.
Lief Eric who?
Lief Eric out of the team, he's hopeless!

Knock, knock.
Who's there?
Macho.
Macho who?
I always watch Macho' the Day.

Knock, knock.
Who's there?
Thermos.
Thermos who?
Thermos be a better team than this!

Knock, knock.
Who's there?
Mayonnaise.
Mayonnaise who?
Mayonnaise have seen what the ref's haven't!

Knock, knock.
Who's there?
Aardvark.
Aardvark who?
Aardvark all the way to Scotland to see
Celtic play.

Knock, knock.
Who's there?
Wanda.
Wanda who?
Wanda buy a new football?

Knock, knock.
Who's there?
Dozen.
Dozen who?
Dozen anyone in this village play football?

Knock, knock.
Who's there?
Gladys.
Gladys who?
Gladys Saturday – we can go to the match.

Knock, knock.
Who's there?
Justin.
Justin who?
Justin time to see us lose!

Knock, knock.
Who's there?
Stan.
Stan who?
Stan back, I'm going to shoot!

Knock, knock.
Who's there?
Philippa.
Philippa who?
Philippa bath tub, I'm covered in mud.

Knock, knock.
Who's there?
Willy.
Willy who?
Willy score? Bet he won't!

Knock, knock.
Who's there?
Tyrone.
Tyrone who?
Tyrone bootlaces.

Knock, knock.
Who's there?
Wayne.
Wayne who?
Wayne never stops when I play football.

Knock, knock.
Who's there?
Snow.
Snow who?
Snow use, I'm going to give you a red
card.

Knock, knock.
Who's there?
Norma Lee.
Norma Lee who?
Norma Lee I play in goal but today I'm at left back.

Knock, knock.
Who's there?
N.E.
N.E. who?
N.E. body could play better than you!

Knock, knock.
Who's there?
Althea.
Althea who?
Althea later, down the club.

Knock, knock.
Who's there?
Buster.
Buster who?
Buster Old Trafford, please.

Knock, knock.
Who's there?
Ivan.
Ivan who?
Ivan new pair of boots, do you like them?

Knock, knock.
Who's there?
Anatole.
Anatole who?
Anatole me you're a hopeless player.

Knock, knock.
Who's there?
Ben.
Ben who?
Ben playing football today, have you?

Knock, knock.
Who's there?
Colin.
Colin who?
Colin and see me after the match.

Knock, knock.
Who's there?
Yolande.
Yolande who?
Yolande me some money to get into the
    match and I'll pay you back next week.

Knock, knock.
Who's there?
Mister.
Mister who?
Mister bus, that's why I'm late for the match.

Knock, knock.
Who's there?
Anna.
Anna who?
Annarack keeps you warm after football.

Knock, knock.
Who's there?
Hammond.
Hammond who?
Hammond eggs are great after football.

45

Knock, knock.
Who's there?
Gorilla.
Gorilla who?
Gorilla the sausages so we can eat before the match.

Knock, knock.
Who's there?
Harriet.
Harriet who?
Harriet all my sandwiches, now I'm too weak to play!

Half-Time

Take a quick break from the golden game to catch up on your reading. Here are some of the titles in the club library.

Embarrassing Moments on the Pitch by Lucy Lastic
Twenty-five Years in Goal by Annie Versary
Willie Win by Betty Wont
Let the Game Begin by Sally Forth
The Unhappy Fan by Mona Lott
The Poor Striker by Miss D. Goal
Why I Gave Up Football by Arthur Itis
Keep Trying Until the Final Whistle by Percy Vere
Heading the Ball by I.C. Starrs
We'll Win the Cup by R.U. Sure
Pre-Match Night Nerves by Eliza Wake
Keep Your Subs Handy by Justin Case
Training Hard by Xavier Strength
Buying Good Players by Ivor Fortune
The New Player by Izzy Anygood
Great Shot! by Major Runn
Advertising the Match by Bill Poster
Half-time Drinks by R.E. Volting

Which soccer manager is found in the greengrocer's?
Terry Vegetables.

Which famous Liverpool player was a sweeper?
Ian Brush.

DAD: Your school report is terrible. You've come
bottom out of 30 in every subject – you're even
bottom in football, and that's your favourite.
SON: It could be worse.
DAD: How?
**SON: I'd be bottom out of 50 if I were in John's
class, it's bigger.**

A young football fan of Southend
Wrote in rhyme – several verses he penned,
Of their triumphs and glory,
Their total history –
It drove all his friends round the bend.

A young football fan from Quebec
Once wrapped both his feet round his neck.
Though he tried hard, he got
Tied up in a knot,
And now he's an absolute wreck.

What's the best day for a footballer to eat bacon and eggs for breakfast?
Fry-day.

DAVE: Did you manage to mend my football game, Dad?
DAD: It wasn't broken – it was just the battery was flat.
DAVE: What shape should it be?

FIRST FOOTBALLER: I received an anonymous letter today.
SECOND FOOTBALLER: Really? Who was it from?

FIRST FOOTBALLER: That dog's useless.
SECOND FOOTBALLER: How do you mean?
FIRST FOOTBALLER: I was watering the pitch yesterday and he never lifted a leg to help me.

Why did the footballer's dog run away from home?
Doggone if I know!

ERIC: My doctor says I can't play football.
DEREK: Oh, so he's seen you play, too, has he?

Why did the man become a marathon runner instead of a footballer?
The doctor told him he had athlete's foot.

A kind lady found a little boy sitting crying on the pavement. 'What's the matter, young man?' she asked.

'It's my birthday,' sobbed the lad. 'And I got a new football, and some boots, and a Manchester United shirt, and a video, and . . . '

'If you got all those lovely things, why are you crying?' asked the lady.

'I'm lost,' sniffed the boy.

MAGGIE: That football player annoys me.
AGGIE: But he's not even looking at you.
MAGGIE: That's what's annoying me!

FOOTBALLER: Two pork chops, please, and make them lean.
WAITER: Certainly, sir. Which way?

Why did the footballer call his cat Ben Hur?
It was just called Ben until it had kittens.

Why did the footballer call his dog Carpenter?
He was always doing little jobs around the house.

Two boys were walking past a house surrounded by a high wall when the owner came out holding a football. 'Is this your ball?' he demanded.

'Er, has it done any damage?' asked the first boy.

'No,' said the householder.

'Then it's ours,' said the second boy.

What position did Cinderella play in the football team?
Sweeper.

Why was Cinderella thrown out of the football team?
Because she kept running away from the ball.

Why did the thief who broke into the football club and stole all the entrance money take a shower before he left?
So he could make a clean getaway.

Did you hear about the footballer who had to lose weight? He went on a coconut and banana diet. He didn't lose any weight, but he couldn't half climb trees!

LARGE FOOTBALLER: My doctor put me on a seafood diet.
SMALL FOOTBALLER: Really?
LARGE FOOTBALLER: Yes. Whenever I see food I eat it.

Why did the doctor write on the footballer's toes?
To add a footnote.

SICK FOOTBALLER: Doctor, will these little blue pills really make me a better player?
DOCTOR: I don't know, but no one I've given them to has ever come back.

DOCTOR: How's your broken rib?
FOOTBALLER: I keep getting a stitch in my side.
DOCTOR: That's good, it shows the bones are knitting.

BOSS: I thought you wanted the afternoon off to see your dentist.
MR BROWN: That's right.
BOSS: Then how come I saw you leaving the football ground with a friend?
MR BROWN: That was my dentist.

MUM: Was there a fight at the match? You've lost your front teeth.
TOMMY: No I haven't. They're in my pocket.

A house was on fire, and a fireman called up a woman trapped on the upper floor to throw down the baby she was holding.

'I can't, you might drop him,' screamed the woman.

'I won't, I used to be a professional footballer,' yelled the fireman.

So the woman threw down the baby, and the fireman headed him over the garden wall.

Two fleas were leaving a football match when it started to rain. 'Shall we walk?' asked the first flea.

'No,' said the second, 'let's take a dog.'

What did the football say to the player?
'I get a kick out of you.'

How can you tell when a footballer has a glass eye?
When it comes out in conversation.

It was Christmas time, and a little boy was being asked by his teacher about the Three Wise Men.

'Who were they?' asked the teacher.

'They were footballers,' replied the little boy.

'Whatever do you mean?' asked the teacher.

'Well, the carol says, **'We three kings of Orient are . . .'**

Which footballer can jump higher than a house?
All of them – houses can't jump.

MRS GREEN: My husband's found a hobby he can stick to at last.
MRS WHITE: What's that?
MRS GREEN: He spends all evening glued to the football on TV.

LEN: Did you hear about the Italian footballer who belonged to a secret society that beat people up with shopping baskets?
KEN: No!
LEN: Yes. He was a member of the Raffia.

PARK-KEEPER: Why are you boys playing football in the trees?
BILLY AND WILLY: Because the sign says no ball games on the grass.

What does a footballer lose every time he stands up?
His lap.

FIRST FOOTBALLER: Did you enjoy your massage?
SECOND FOOTBALLER: Oh yes. I like to feel kneaded.

How did the Japanese soccer millionaire make all his money?
He had a yen for that kind of thing.

Where can a fan stop for a drink when he's driving to the match?
At a T-junction.

What was wrong with the footballer whose nose ran and whose feet smelt?
He was built upside down.

FOOTBALLER: I've a terrible pain in my right foot. What should I do?
PHYSIOTHERAPIST: Kick the ball with your left foot.

DAD: You must have a goal in life.
SON: OK, I'll join the local football club.

Why do ghosts play football?
For the ghouls, of course.

Who delivers mail to footballers?
The goal-post man.

What do you call a press photographer taking pictures of the match?
A flash guy.

Did you hear the story of the peacock who played football?
It was a beautiful tail.

What's the easiest way to find a broken bottle on the football pitch?
Play in your bare feet.

Own Goal

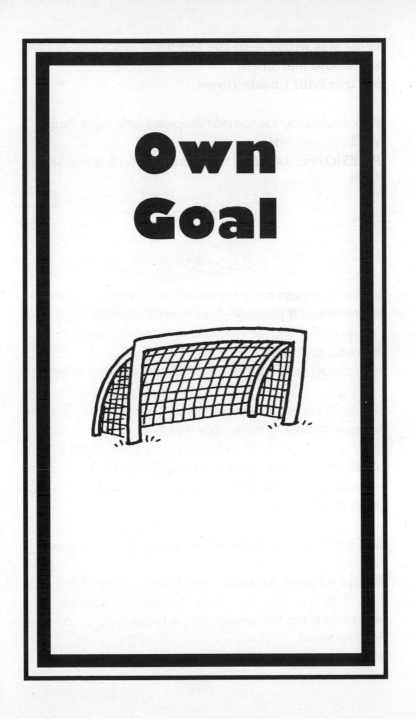

GARY: I'm sorry I missed the goal. I could kick myself, I really could.
BARRY: Don't bother – you'd miss.

'May I have your autograph?' a small boy asked a footballer outside the ground.

Trying to get away from him, the footballer lied, 'I really don't play football.'

'I know,' said the boy. 'But I'd like your autograph anyway.'

Sammy skived off school, saying he was going to his grandfather's funeral. Unfortunately one of his teachers recognized him at the local football match, where the score was 8–0 to the visiting side.

'So this is your grandfather's funeral?' asked the teacher.

'Looks like it,' replied the boy. 'That's him in goal.'

Young Jimmy was nervous when he first played for the team, and when they stopped for half-time he asked the captain, 'I suppose you've seen worse players.'

The captain scratched his head.

'I said, I suppose you've seen worse players,' persisted Jimmy.

'I heard you the first time,' replied the captain. 'I was just trying to remember.'

Old Butterfingers had let five goals through in the first half. 'Can you lend me 50p?' he asked the captain. 'I want to phone a friend.'

'Here's £1,' said the captain. 'Phone all your friends.'

GOALKEEPER: Doctor, I can't sleep at night.
DOCTOR: *How long has this been going on?*
GOALKEEPER: About a year.
DOCTOR: *You haven't slept for a year?*
GOALKEEPER: I can sleep during the matches, but not at night.

It was a cold, wet, miserable day and the goalie had had a bad match, allowing several goals through. As he sat moping in the dressing room, he sniffed and muttered, 'I think I've caught a cold.'

'Thank goodness you can catch something,' said the captain.

TRAINER: You must work hard at your fitness training, Andrews. Remember, hard work never killed anyone.
ANDREWS: *No, and I'm not going to be the first!*

FIRST FOOTBALLER: How did you manage to break your leg?
SECOND FOOTBALLER: *See those steps down to the car park?*
FIRST FOOTBALLER: Yes
SECOND FOOTBALLER: *I didn't.*

The team kept losing, but the captain shrugged off their run of bad luck. 'After all, what's defeat?'

'What you're supposed to kick the ball with,' answered one of the players.

The goalie was so short-sighted he couldn't see the ball until it was too late. A doctor friend prescribed carrots to help his eyesight.

The goalie ate lots of carrots, but he went back to the doctor a week later, saying he still couldn't catch the ball because now every time he moved he tripped over his ears.

What gloves can a goalie see and smell but not wear?
Foxgloves.

What's the difference between a gutter and a poor goalie?
One catches drops; the other drops catches.

What do you get if you cross a gorilla with a footballer?
I don't know, but when it tries to score a goal no one tries to stop it!

What's the difference between a goalie who's asleep and one who's awake?
With some goalies it's difficult to tell!

Why is it important to a goalie that you spell words correctly?
Because if you reverse the letters in the middle of GOAL he'd spend his time in GAOL.

FOOTBALLER: You should be ashamed, giving me such a poultry salary.
MANAGER: You mean 'paltry'.
FOOTBALLER: No, I mean 'poultry' – it's chicken feed.

UP-AND-COMING FOOTBALLER: I've been told I have music in my feet.
VETERAN FOOTBALLER: Yes, two flats!

Did you hear about the retiring footballer who bought a paper shop?
It blew away.

Why did the idiot come on the pitch dressed in diving gear?
He'd been told he might be needed as a sub.

When is a footballer in hospital with a broken leg a contradiction?
When he's an impatient patient.

Did you hear about the player who threw away his boots because he thought they were sticking out their tongues at him?

FIRST PLAYER: Why is your arm in a sling?
SECOND PLAYER: I get all the breaks.

FIRST PLAYER: I take a dim view of that captain's tactics.
SECOND PLAYER: That's because you've forgotten to take your shades off.

SUSIE: Why don't you like your new football coach?
SIMON: Because he told me to play in goal for the present, and he didn't give me a present!

FOOTBALLER, TO PSYCHIATRIST: I can't run, can't shoot, can't dribble, and I'm no good in goal.
PSYCHIATRIST: Why don't you give up football?
FOOTBALLER: I can't, I'm the team captain.

One player was the despair of the coach. Everything he did was wrong, until finally he got a perfect chance at goal. 'Shoot! Shoot!' yelled the coach.

The player looked round in bewilderment. 'But I haven't got a gun,' he replied.

GOALIE: Where shall we put the new player?
CAPTAIN: What's his name?
GOALIE: Robin Swallow.
CAPTAIN: Put him on the wing.

CAPTAIN: Why are you late for training?
PLAYER: I sprained my ankle.
CAPTAIN: That's a lame excuse.

NICK: How old is your goalie?
MICK: Approaching 30.
NICK: From which direction?

DANNY: Did you hear about the overweight player whose doctor put him on a diet that used a lot of olive oil?
ANNIE: Did he lose weight?
DANNY: No, but his knees don't creak any more.

Why did the daft goalie take a tape measure to bed with him?
To find out how long he slept.

A weedy little man wanted to get fit enough to play football, so he bought a big book on body building and worked hard on the exercises for three months. A friend asked him if it had had any effect.
'Certainly,' he replied. 'I can now lift up the book.'

What does a goalie have when he doesn't feel well?
Gloves on his hands.

FIRST PLAYER: 'That trainer's a real angel.'
SECOND PLAYER: 'Yes, he does harp on about things, doesn't he?'

VETERAN FOOTBALLER: How old are you?
SECOND VETERAN FOOTBALLER: Thirty-two.
But I don't look it, do I?
FIRST VETERAN FOOTBALLER: No, but you used to.

Two young footballers were talking about the illnesses and accidents they had had.

'Once I couldn't walk for a year,' said the first.

'When was that?' asked the other.

'When I was a baby,' replied the first.

What did the poor footballer say when the substitute changed places with him?
'What a relief!'

P.E. TEACHER: Now, Billy, you promised to practise hard at your football, didn't you?
BILLY: Yes.
P.E. TEACHER: And I promised to punish you if you didn't practise?
BILLY: Yes. But I don't mind if you break your promise.

Why was the goalie fired?
He was so gentle he wouldn't even catch a fly.

Nobody ever passed the ball to Willie, and he was moaning in the dressing room that he might as well be invisible.

'Who said that?' asked the captain.

Old Harry had been retired from the game for many years, but he still liked to tell people how good he'd once been. 'They still remember me, you know,' he said. 'Only yesterday, when I was at the players' entrance, there were lots of press photographers queuing to take my picture.

'Really?' said a disbelieving listener.

'Yes. And if you don't believe me, ask Michael Owen – he was standing next to me.'

It was a warm day for football and the striker kept missing his shots. At half-time he said, 'What couldn't I do with a long, cold drink.'

His captain looked at him thoughtfully. 'Kick it?' he asked.

The goalie played a dreadful match, not managing to save one ball. During the week he practised very hard for the following weekend's game. 'Notice any difference?' he asked the captain.

The captain looked at him for a few minutes before replying, 'Yes. You've shaved off your beard.'

What's higher than an Italian football captain?
His cap.

The great goalkeeper Jim 'Big Hands' O'Reilly was walking down the street. 'I recognize that man,' said Ken. 'But what's his name?'

'That's Big Hands,' replied Ben.

'Oh, really?'

'No, O'Reilly.'

Who's in goal when the ghost team plays football?
The ghoulie, of course!

Which famous Manchester United manager was like a Buckingham Palace guardsman who'd been run over by a steamroller?
Flat Busby.

Which footballer ate his food very quickly?
Bruce Gobblehard.

A footballer was fond of going for long walks to help himself keep fit. 'Every day,' he said to his friend, 'my dog and I go for a tramp in the woods.'

'Does the dog enjoy it too?' asked the friend.

'Yes,' replied the footballer, 'but the tramp's getting a bit fed up.'

Why was there a piano in the players' showers?
So they could play Handel's Water Music.

CONCEITED PLAYER: I don't like this photo of me – it doesn't do me justice.
OTHER PLAYER: It's mercy you want, not justice.

ANGRY NEIGHBOUR: Didn't you hear me banging on your wall last night?
BLEARY-EYED NEIGHBOUR: That's all right – we had a bit of a party after the match and we were making quite a lot of noise ourselves.

What belongs to a footballer but is used more by other people?
His name.

How can a footballer make more of his money?
If he folds up a note he'll find it in creases.

Why did the millionaire footballer have no bathroom in his house?
He was filthy rich.

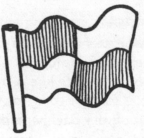

DARREN: Did you hear about the footballer who ate little bits of metal all day?
SHARON: No.
DARREN: It was his staple diet.

Two footballers were about to retire. 'There's only one way of making money honestly,' said the first.
    'What's that?' asked the second.
    'I might have known that you wouldn't know,' retorted the first.

OLD FOOTBALL FAN: At last I've got my new hearing aid.

FRIEND: Does it work well?

OLD FAN: Half-past three.

DANIEL: Mum, can I go out and play?

MUM: What, with those holes in your socks?

DANIEL: No, with Billy next door. He's got a new football.

WAYNE: Why didn't you put a knife and fork on the table for your brother when you laid the table?

JANE: Because Mum said that when he's been playing football he eats like a horse.

Who runs out on the pitch when a player is injured and says, 'Miaow'?

The first-aid kit.

POLICEMAN: I'm sorry, but I'm going to have to lock you up for the night.

UNRULY FAN: What's the charge?

POLICEMAN: There's no charge, it's all part of the service.

Kitbag

What did the left football boot say to the right football boot?
'Between us we should have a ball.'

Why do footballers wear shorts?
Because they'd be arrested if they didn't.

Who wears the biggest boots in the England team?
The player with the biggest feet.

MUM: You've got your boots on the wrong feet.
YOUNG ALEC: But, Mum, these are the only feet I've got.

Why can't a car play football?
Because it's only got one boot.

What do jelly babies wear on their feet when they play football?
Gumboots.

TERRY: I bought one of those new paper shirts last week.
KERRY: What's it like?
TERRY: Tear-able.

HARRY: What kind of leather makes the best football boots?
LARRY: *I don't know, but banana peel makes the best slippers.*

MUM: Why are you crying?
TIMMY: *Jimmy's lost his football boots.*
MUM: But if he's lost his boots, why are you crying?
TIMMY: *Because I was wearing them when he lost them.*

What's the difference between an oak tree and a tight football boot?
One makes acorns, the other makes corns ache.

What did the boy do when his aunt sent him a football shirt for his birthday that was much too small?
He wrote her a short thank-you letter, saying he would have written more but he was all choked up.

MICKY: My brother's away, training to be in a football team.
NICKY: Lucky thing! He must be quite grown up now.
MICKY: Yes. He wrote the other day saying he'd grown another foot, so my mum is knitting him an extra sock.

Dim Dennis went to a factory where football boots were made. 'What do you make them from?' he asked.

'Hide,' replied the factory manager.

'Why, who's coming?' asked the boy.

BOB: I can't find my football boots, and I've looked everywhere for them.
TEACHER: Are you sure these aren't yours? They're the only pair left.
BOB: Quite sure. Mine had snow on them.

A father asked his son what he'd like for Christmas. 'I've got my eye on that special football in the sports shop window,' replied the lad.

'The £50 one?' asked his dad.

'That's right,' replied his son.

'You'd better keep your eye on it — 'cos it's unlikely your boot will ever kick it,' said his dad firmly.

The footballer had been hit very hard on his knee, which had swollen up enormously. 'If it gets bigger I won't be able to get my shorts on,' he told the doctor.

'Don't worry, I'll write you a prescription,' said the doctor.

'What for?'

'A skirt.'

ANDY: Do you have holes in your football shorts?
BERTIE: No.
ANDY: Then how do you get them on?

What wears out football boots but has no feet?
The ground.

Why did the footballer put corn in his boots?
He had pigeon toes.

Young Chris was sent home from school for not bringing his football kit. When he returned in the afternoon he was wet through.

'Why are you all wet?' asked the P.E. teacher.

'Sir, you said I had to play football in my sports kit, so I went home to fetch it, but it was all in the wash.'

When do a footballer's swimming trunks go ding dong?
When he wrings them out.

What did the football sock say to the football boot?
'Well, I'll be darned!'

FIRST SPIDER: I don't know what to get my husband for Christmas.
SECOND SPIDER: Do what I did – get him four pairs of football boots.

How short can a footballer's shorts get?
They'll always be above two feet.

SIGN ON A NEW SPORTS KIT SHOP:
Don't go elsewhere to be robbed – try us first!

Why does a professional footballer always put his right boot on first?
It would be silly to put the wrong boot on, wouldn't it?

What runs around all day and lies at night with its tongue hanging out?
A football boot.

OLDER BROTHER: Have you got your football boots on yet?
YOUNGER BROTHER: Yes, all but one.

BOB: I wish I were in your boots.
ROB: Why?
BOB: Mine have holes in them.

FREDDIE: Why have you got your football socks on inside out?
TEDDIE: There are holes on the outside.

Why are a pair of much-worn football socks like a taxi driver?
They both drive you away.

GILES: What's a football made of?
MILES: Pig's hide.
GILES: Why do they hide?
MILES: No – the pig's outside.
GILES: Then bring him in. Any friend of yours is a friend of mine.

ANGRY CAPTAIN: You should have been here at 9.30.
LATE PLAYER: Why, what happened?

FIRST FOOTBALLER: Do you think it will rain for the match this afternoon?
SECOND FOOTBALLER: That depends on the weather, doesn't it?

What does a footballer part with but never give away?
His comb!

What can a footballer keep even if he does give it away?
A cold!

INSURANCE AGENT: This is a very good policy, sir. We pay up to £1000 for broken arms and legs.
DUMB FOOTBALLER: But what do you do with them all?

Why did the footballer stand on his head?
He was turning things over in his mind.

Why did the football coach have to wear sunglasses?
Because his pupils were so bright.

What's the cheapest time to phone a footballer?
When he's out!

TERRY: It's true that TV causes violence.
JERRY: Why do you say that?
TERRY: Because every time I switch on the match my mum hits me.

Why was the snowman no good playing in the big match?
He got cold feet.

Why did the bald footballer throw away his keys?
He'd lost all his locks.

How long does an Italian player cook spaghetti?
About 20 centimetres.

How does an Italian player eat spaghetti?
He puts it in his mouth.

Why did the conceited player throw a bucket of water on the pitch when he made his debut?
He wanted to make a big splash.

What does a footballer do if he splits his sides laughing?
Runs until he gets a stitch.

FIRST FOOTBALLER: When is it your birthday?
SECOND FOOTBALLER: 2nd June.
FIRST FOOTBALLER: Which year?
SECOND FOOTBALLER: Every year.

A group of neighbours were organizing a village friendly match, followed by a picnic, and realized they'd forgotten to invite the eccentric old lady who lived on the green. So they sent a child to invite her.

'It's no use now,' said the old lady, 'I've already prayed for rain.'

MOTHER: Why are you taking the baby's bib out with you, Tommy? I thought you were going to football practice?
TOMMY: Yes, but the coach said we'd be dribbling this week.

TRAFFIC WARDEN: Why did you park your car there?
FOOTBALL FAN: Because the notice says 'Fine for parking'.

FIRST EXCITED FOOTBALL FAN: Let's take some fruit into the living room when we watch *Match of the Day*.
SECOND FOOTBALL FAN: Why?
FIRST FAN: Because I want to eat strawberries and scream!

What happens if you wrap your sandwiches in your favourite comic when you go to football practice?
You get crumby jokes!

DAFT FOOTBALLER: Do you remember when I came to see you about my rheumatism and you told me to stay away from damp places?
DOCTOR: Yes.
DAFT FOOTBALLER: Well, it's much better now, so can I start having baths again?

Two boys were trespassing on the local football pitch and the groundsman came out and bellowed at them. 'Didn't you see that sign?' he yelled.

'Yes, but it said "Private" at the top so we didn't like to read any further,' replied the boys.

WAYNE: Did you hear that the police are searching the football crowd for a man with one eye called McTavish?
JANE: What's his other eye called?

A fan driving at 120 mph so he wouldn't arrive late at the match was stopped by the police. 'Oh dear,' he said, 'was I driving too fast?'

'No, sir,' said the officer. 'Flying too low.'

Two fans were discussing their packed lunches. 'What have you got?' asked the first.

'Tongue sandwiches,' the other replied.

'Ugh, I couldn't eat something that had come out of an animal's mouth.'

'What have you got, then?' asked the second fan.

'Egg sandwiches.'

P. E. TEACHER: Now, Clarence, I'm trying to tell you how to make a tackle. I wish you'd pay a little attention.
CLARENCE: I'm paying as little as I can.

GLEN: I had an argument with my sister. I wanted to watch football on TV and she wanted to watch a film.
BEN: What film did you see?

ANGRY NEIGHBOUR: I'll teach you to kick footballs in my greenhouse!
NAUGHTY BOY: I wish you would – I keep missing!

What happens to football fans who eat too many sweets?
They take up two seats.

Final Whistle

'Doctor, doctor, I feel like a referee.'
'So do I – let's go and buy a couple at the corner shop.'

What was the film about referees called?
The Umpire Strikes Back.

If you have a referee in football and an umpire in cricket, what do you have in bowls?
Goldfish.

What happened when the referee had a brain transplant?
The brain rejected him.

When is a trainer like a bird of prey?
When he watches you like a hawk.

What do you call a referee wearing five balaclavas on a cold day?
Anything you like, he can't hear you.

KIM: Did you say that the referee spreads happiness wherever he goes?
JIM: No, I said whenever he goes.

'Off!' shouted the ref, blowing his whistle.
'Off? What for?' asked the player.
'For the rest of the match,' replied the ref.

Who hangs out the washing on a football pitch?
The linesman.

Why did the referee have a sausage stuck behind his ear?
Because he'd eaten his whistle at lunch-time.

MR BLACK: Our lad's so dumb he thinks a football coach has four wheels!
MR WHITE: Why, how many does it have?

When is a football coach not a football coach?
When it turns into the ground.

A football coach driver went to a garage. 'Can you have a look at my bus? I think the engine's flooded,' he told the mechanic.
    'Is it on the road outside?' asked the garage man.
    'No, it's at the bottom of the canal,' replied the coach driver.

Why did the football coach driver drive his coach in reverse?
Because he knew the Highway Code backwards.

Which part of a football coach is the laziest?
The wheels – they're always tyred.

BEN: Our team's just bought a baby coach to carry us from match to match.
LEN: A baby coach?
BEN: Yes. It doesn't go anywhere without a rattle.

DARREN: When I grow up I want to drive a football coach.
DAD: OK, son, I won't stand in your way.

TED: Have you heard about Mrs Brown? She's left her husband and gone off with the football coach!
NED: I didn't even know she could drive!

'Doctor! Come quickly! The referee has swallowed his biro! What can we do?'
'Use another one until I get there.'

DONNY: I've never refereed a football match before. Do I have to run after the ball?
RONNIE: No, after the match.

CLAUDE: But for Herbert we'd have lost the match today.
MAUD: *Is he the striker or the goalie?*
CLAUDE: Neither – he's the ref.

The devil proposed a soccer match between heaven and hell. 'That wouldn't be fair,' said an imp. 'Heaven has all the footballers.'

'I know,' replied the devil. 'But we have all the referees.'

Did you hear about the referee who got so fed up with the bad players in the teams playing that he awarded a free kick to himself?

Did you hear about the referee who was so short-sighted he couldn't go to sleep unless he counted elephants?

The referee was showing his friends his new stopwatch. 'It's an amazing watch,' he said. 'It only cost 50p.'

'Why is it so amazing?'

'Because every time I look at it I'm amazed it's still working.'

One day when United were playing, the referee didn't turn up, so the captain asked if there was anyone among the spectators with refereeing experience. A man stepped forward.

'Have you refereed before?' asked the captain.

'Certainly,' said the man. 'And if you don't believe me, ask my three friends here.'

'I'm sorry,' said the captain. 'But I don't think we can use you.'

'Why not?'

'You can't be a real referee because no real referee has three friends.'

Why is a referee like a kettle?
They both whistle when they're hot.

Which footballer keeps the house warm in winter?
Andy Coal (Cole).

REFEREE: Will I be able to see right across the pitch
with these new glasses?
OPTICIAN: Yes.
REFEREE: That's wonderful! I never could with the old
ones.

Three footballers got caught out in the snow, but only
two got their hair wet. Why?
The other one was bald!

Why is a football crowd learning to sing like a person
trying to get into the wrong house?
They both have trouble with the key.

ANNIE: How long were you in the school football
team?
DANNY: About 137 centimetres.

A lad going home from playing football in the park saw a beautiful new car parked up the road from his house. He bounced the ball on and off its bumpers, but when he bounced it on the windscreen the glass smashed in pieces. The boy's father, who was coming to collect him, saw what happened, and shouted angrily, 'Didn't I tell you? If you burst that football I'm not buying you another!'

LOU: Do you like the new captain?
HUGH: I can't complain. Let's face it, I daren't!

DAD: Shall I put the kettle on?
SON: You could, but I think you look all right in your football kit.

FIRST FOOTBALLER: The new player isn't up to much.
SECOND FOOTBALLER: I think we should take him at face value.
FIRST FOOTBALLER: With his face, that doesn't amount to very much.

FIRST FOOTBALLER: Girls whisper that they love me.
SECOND FOOTBALLER: Well, they'd never admit it out loud!

REFEREE: I didn't come here to be insulted!
DISGRUNTLED FAN: Where do you usually go?

FATHER: You mustn't fight, you must learn to give and take.
DENNIS: I did. I gave Danny a black eye and took his football!

FIRST FOOTBALLER: That ointment the doctor gave me to rub on my knee makes my hands smart.
SECOND FOOTBALLER: Then why don't you rub some into your head?

BILLY: That new striker's a man who's going places!
WILLY: And the sooner the better!

BEN: I hear that new player's father is an optician.
LEN: Is that why he keeps making such a spectacle of himself?

FIRST FOOTBALLER: My girlfriend's really clever. She has brains enough for two.
SECOND FOOTBALLER: Then she's obviously the girl for you!

MOTHER TO MUDDY FOOTBALLING DAUGHTER: You're pretty dirty, Bobbie.
BOBBIE: I'm even prettier clean.

BILL: That coach always thinks twice before speaking.
PHIL: Yes, so he can think up something really nasty to say!

HARRY: Our captain is a man with polish.
LARRY: Only on his boots!

Ned was speaking about the opposing team's striker. 'He's out of this world!' he said.

Ted grinned wryly. 'Our team often wishes he were.'

JERRY: That goalie looks very heavy, but they say he's a light eater.
TERRY: *He is. As soon as it's light he starts eating.*

Sally and Susie were discussing a particularly good-looking soccer star. 'Do you think he's conceited?' asked Sally.

'Who else has a mirror on the bathroom ceiling so he can watch himself gargle?' replied Susie.

Why didn't the conceited star wash very often?
Because when the bathroom mirror got all steamed up he couldn't admire himself!

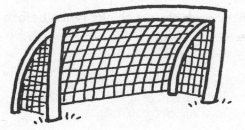

How can you make a tall footballer short?
Ask him to lend you all his money.

United had been playing badly and their manager hired a hall in which to hold a press conference.

Afterwards, Bill said to Gill, 'Did you notice how the manager's voice filled the hall?'

'Yes,' she replied. 'And did you notice how many people left to make room for it?'

A man realized that his new neighbour was a famous football player. 'I've seen you on the TV, on and off,' he said.

'And how do you like me?' asked the player.

'Off,' replied his neighbour.

FOOTBALL

by Sandy Ransford

Illustrated by David Mostyn

FOOTBALL PUZZLES

by Sandy Ransford
Illustrated by David Mostyn

Contents

Rules of the Game

1 How many players are there in a soccer team?

2 Who in the team can handle the ball?

3 With which parts of their bodies may players move the ball?

4 How many referee's assistants are there?

5 How do the referee's assistants signal to the referee?

6 How many substitutes are allowed in a game of football?

7 How long is each half of play?

8 How long is the half-time interval?

9 What does the ball have to do for a goal to be scored?

10 If the ball stops on the touchline, is it out of play?

11 What is an indirect free kick?

12 If a player takes a corner kick, how far away from him must his opponent be?

13 How much should a football weigh?

14 What must a goalkeeper wear?

15 Can the ball be changed during the game?

Afternoon Out

It's Saturday afternoon and you're off to the match. But how good are you at working out what your money will buy?

1 If your bus fare is 80p each way, and it costs £10 to get into the ground, and you spend 50p on a drink when you're there, how many 2p sweets can you buy on the way home if you started out with £13?

2 If the ground holds 50,000 people, and it is 65 per cent full, how many people are at the match?

3 If, on your way home, you decide you don't want any sweets, but, together with your friend, you'd like some fish and chips, how much money would you have to borrow from your friend if a portion of fish is £1.20 and a portion of chips is 85p?

Woolly Mufflers

How many football scarves can you spot in the picture?

Picture Puzzle

This crossword has both picture and word clues, so you should find it easy to solve.

Across

1 There are two at the goal (4)
5 Game (5)
6 A _ _ _ _ _ _ kick is taken from the quarter circle by the flag (6)
7 All 11 players (4)
9 He might be a right or a left (4)
10 Picture Clue (3)
12 Picture Clue (4)
14 What you do with the ball (4)
16 Picture Clue (10)
18 Picture Clue (7)
21 Picture Clue (4)
22 Queen's _ _ _ _ Rangers (4)
23 Association football (6)
24 Picture Clue (7)

Down

2 Picture Clue (5)
3 Picture Clue (4)
4 It's at right angles to the goal line (9)
7 Intercept player with ball (6)
8 A penalty kick is taken from the penalty _ _ _ _ (4)
11 Picture Clue (4)
13 Another name for a mid-fielder (4-3)
15 Picture Clue (8)
16 The aim of the game (4)
17 Another name for a forward (7)
19 Picture Clue (6)
20 Picture Clue (5)

ACROSS

WORN UNDER SOCK
10(3)

24(7)

18(7)

16(10)

21(4)

12(4)

DOWN

2(5)

3(4)

11(4)

19(6)

20(5)

15(8)

First Half

How many differences can you spot between these two scenes of a match?

Name-dropping

Listed below are the names of some very well-known players of the past, both British and international, but the letters have been jumbled up. Can you work out who they are?

1 JEVION NINES

2 COAL LED RAT RIM

3 NINK JAMS GLEN RUN

4 THROB BABY CLON

5 PAPER JAR PINE IN E

6 GONE MAID ADORA

7 COUG PAGES NAIL

8 LADY G HEN SLINK

9 CAFF JONY HUR

10 GRAB BORE, GI TOO

11 TONI CAN RACE

12 NK RILEY RAGE

Cup Tie

Which of these picturess of the FA Cup is the mirror
image of the top left-hand one?

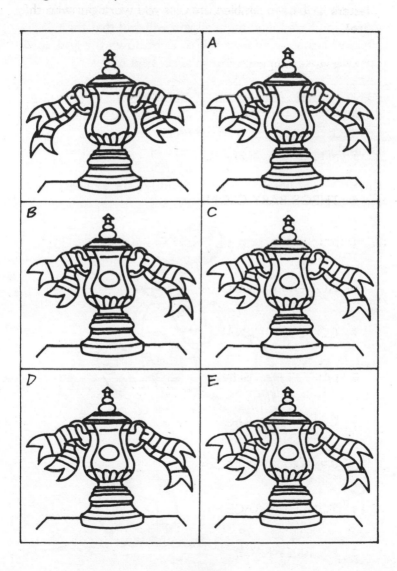

Free Kick

Find all the words listed below in the grid opposite. The words may read across, up, down or diagonally, either forwards or backwards, but they are all in straight lines. When you have found them all you will find that the left-over letters, read from left to right down the grid, spell out two words connected with successful teams.

CENTRE LINE (2 lines)
COACH
DIVING
DRIBBLE
FOUL
KICK OFF (2 lines)
MIDFIELD

OFFSIDE
OWN GOAL (2 lines)
PASS
PITCH
STUD
THROW IN (2 lines)
WING

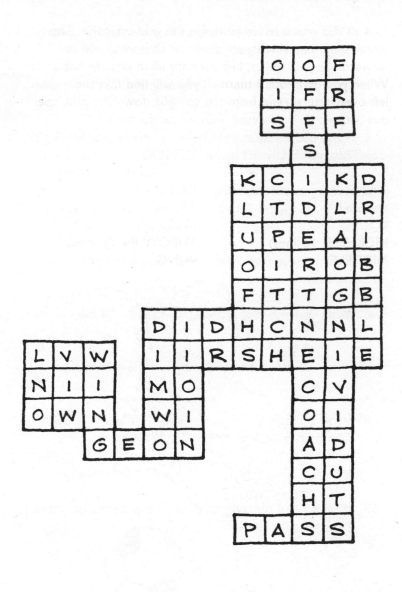

Who or Which?

1 Who replaced Kevin Keegan as manager of Newcastle United in January 1997?

2 Who is Edson Arantes do Nascimento better known as?

3 Who had a statue unveiled in his honour at Benfica's Estadio da Luz in Lisbon in 1992?

4 Who was sold three times for record sums in the early 1980s, led Napoli to their first Italia League title in 1987 and was banned for taking drugs in 1991?

5 Which great Dutch footballer managed both Ajax and Barcelona?

6 Who was the first Englishman to win 100 international caps?

7 Who captained England in their 1966 World Cup victory?

8 Who captained Liverpool when they won the 2005 Champions League Final?

9 Which Spanish team has Michael Owen played for?

10 Which team did Wayne Rooney play for before joining Manchester United?

On the Line

Do you know what these linesman's signals mean?

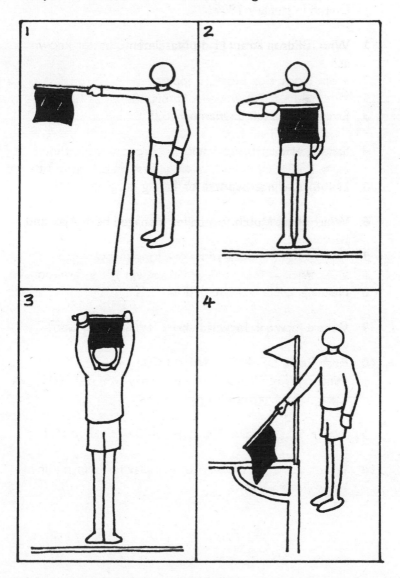

Odd One Out

Circle the odd one out in each of these series of words.

1 Ibrox, Bramall Lane, Hampden Park.

2 Front block, side block, trapping.

3 Juventus, Spartak, Dynamo.

4 Santos, Nacional, Sao Paulo.

5 Link-man, winger, centre striker.

6 Volley, chip, dribble.

7 Out-swinger, underarm throw, long throw.

8 Heading, tripping, obstruction.

9 Centre forward, forward short leg, inside forward.

10 Rose Bowl, UEFA Cup, World Cup.

Knotty Problem

Which laces belong to which boot?

What's in a Name?

Check how much you really know about your favourite game by seeing how many of these technical terms you understand.

 1 Offside.

 2 Free kick.

 3 Foul.

 4 Penalty.

 5 Throw-in.

 6 Yellow card.

 7 Red card.

 8 Flick pass.

 9 Bending.

10 Half volley.

11 Diving.

12 Punching.

What's Missing?

Each of these pictures lacks one detail present in the top left-hand one. Can you spot what it is in each drawing?

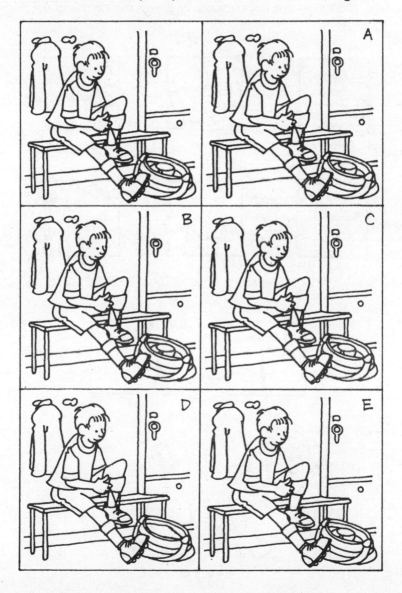

Gridlock

Each of the enlarged squares below matches exactly one of the squares in the picture opposite. Can you spot which they are? They are not necessarily drawn the right way up!

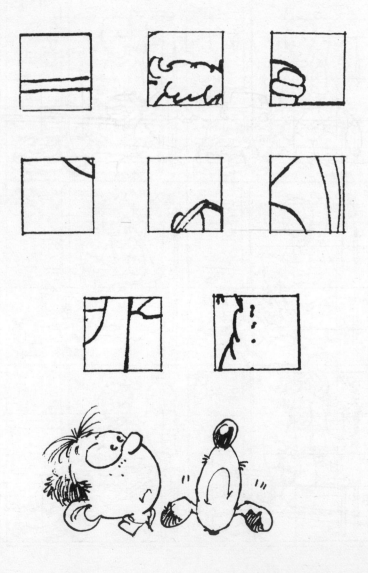

Getting Fit

Solve the clues and enter the answers in the grid. If you solve them correctly you will find, reading down the arrowed column, the name of one of Manchester United's greatest ever players.

1 These exercises are hard work on the arm muscles. (5-3)

2 You might do this on a bike or upside down in the air. (7)

3 If you do too many exercises you might end up like this! (9)

4 You need to do a lot of this up and down the field when playing football. (7)

5 This is a slower version of number 4. (7)

6 All the answers in this puzzle might come under this heading. (8)

7 Propelling yourself through water. (8)

8 Your keep-fit routines need to be this. (7)

9 Keeping fit consists of doing lots of these. (9)

…e these players' positions?

Fill the Gaps

Every other letter is missing from these teams' names. Can you work out what they are? (NB They're all British clubs.)

1 _ E _ D _ _ N _ T _ D

2 I _ B _ E _ O _

3 _ H _ R _ T _ N _ T _ L _ T _ C

4 _ H _ L _ E _

5 _ A _ C _ E _ T _ R _ N _ T _ D

6 _ O _ T _ N _ A _ _ O _ S _ U _

7 _ S _ O _ _ I _ L _

8 _ R _ S _ O _ _ O _ E _ S

9 _ R _ S _ O _ _ O _ T _ _ N _

10 _ A _ T _ C _ _ H _ S _ L _

11 _ E _ B _ _ O _ N _ Y

12 _ O _ V _ R _ A _ P _ O _ _ A _ D _ R _ R _

Odd Picture Out

Which of these six pictures is different from all the others, and why?

Make It Fit

This is a kind of clueless crossword. All you have to do is fit the words below into the grid opposite. Two letters have been given to help you – which should be all you need!

4-letter words
AREA
HALF
TIME
TRIP

5-letter words
BLOCK
BLUES
COACH
EXTRA
FIRST
SCORE
SCOUT
SPEED
SWIFT
UNFIT

6-letter words
ATTACK
LEAGUE

7-letter words
BRITAIN
CAPTAIN
CAUTION
SWEEPER
WINNING

8-letter words
DIVISION
OUTFIELD
TRAINING

9-letter word
TURNSTILE

12-letter word
HANDKERCHIEF

126

Nicknames

Do you recognize these British teams from their nicknames?

1 Minster Men

2 Blades

3 Villans

4 Hammers

5 Pensioners/Blues

6 Potters

7 Gunners

8 Swans

9 Rams

10 Irons

11 Biscuit Men

12 The Bhoys

13 Terrors

14 Lions

15 Stags

How Many?

How many different patterns are there on these footballs?

Word Snake

All the foreign teams listed below can be found in the grid opposite, in the order given. The words form a continuous line, reading up, down, right or left but *not* diagonally. Every letter in the grid is used once only.

AJAX AMSTERDAM

ANDERLECHT

BAYERN MUNICH

BENFICA

BOCA JUNIORS

FEYENOORD

FK AUSTRIA

FLAMENGO

INTERNAZIONALE

MILLONARIOS

PENAROL

REAL MADRID

SPARTA PRAGUE

VASCO DA GAMA

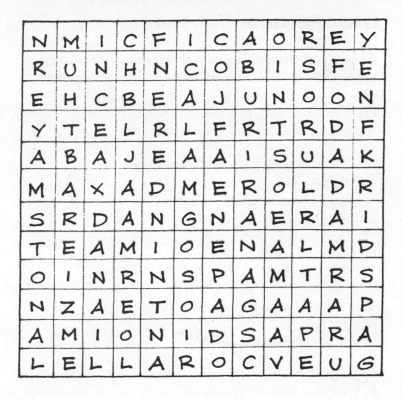

N	M	I	C	F	I	C	A	O	R	E	Y
R	U	N	H	N	C	O	B	I	S	F	E
E	H	C	B	E	A	J	U	N	O	O	N
Y	T	E	L	R	L	F	R	T	R	D	F
A	B	A	J	E	A	A	I	S	U	A	K
M	A	X	A	D	M	E	R	O	L	D	R
S	R	D	A	N	G	N	A	E	R	A	I
T	E	A	M	I	O	E	N	A	L	M	D
O	I	N	R	N	S	P	A	M	T	R	S
N	Z	A	E	T	O	A	G	A	A	A	P
A	M	I	O	N	I	D	S	A	P	R	A
L	E	L	L	A	R	O	C	V	E	U	G

Hidden in a Sentence

A number of 'football' words are hidden in the sentences below. Can you spot them all? Here's an example to help you.

'Is that **man a Ger**man?' (The hidden word is 'manager'.)

1 'Does he wear a cap, T.A., in winter?'

2 'It's a wide fen, Cecil.'

3 'Are the soldiers for war, Daniel?'

4 'Did you show Fifi El Dorado?'

5 'Lift him under the armpit, Charles.'

6 'Don't scoff, Sid Edwards.'

7 'Have you met Tessa Vernon?'

8 'Show Caleb all the pictures, Harry.'

9 'I'm not late, am I?'

10 'Is that a corn, Errol?'

Striking

Which of the strikers pictured below is the one shown above in silhouette?

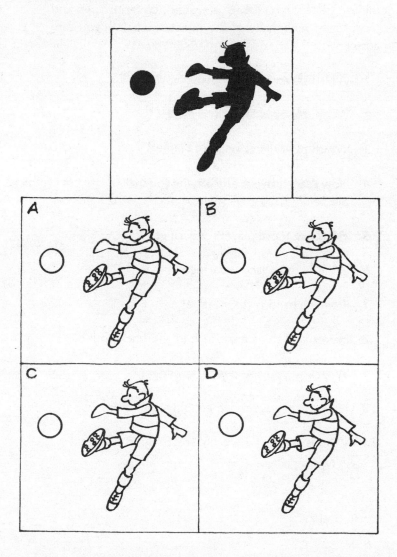

Observation Test

How good are your powers of observation? Test them by looking carefully at the picture opposite for just half a minute (time yourself with a watch), covering it up and then seeing how many of the questions below you can answer.

1   Which player is doing press-ups?

2   Which player is lifting weights?

3   Which player is skipping?

4   How many players are playing football in the corner of the field?

5   What are these players wearing?

6   What is the coach wearing?

7   In which hand is his whistle?

8   How many trees are there in the background?

9   What can you see over the hedge?

10 How many players are running round the field?

11 Who is wearing a woolly scarf round his neck?

Header!

How many differences can you spot between these two pictures of a great header?

Buying Kit

Rich, kind Uncle Henry has given you £100 for your birthday, which you want to spend on the strip of your favourite club. You'd also like a new pair of boots, a pair of socks, and a new football. When you arrive at the shop, you find everything is very expensive, and the boots and football come in a wide range of prices. How can you buy the best you can afford and still have £10 over to spend on a favourite video?

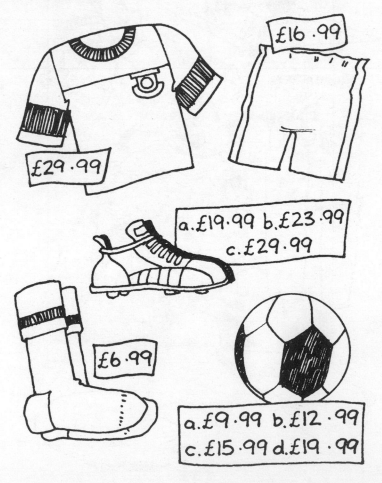

£16.99

£29.99

a. £19.99 b. £23.99
c. £29.99

£6.99

a. £9.99 b. £12.99
c. £15.99 d. £19.99

Rhyme Time

Match the pictures below with the words with which they rhyme.

**BOUGHT   PITCH   CATCH   NOTCH
BRISTLE   GATE   SOCKS**

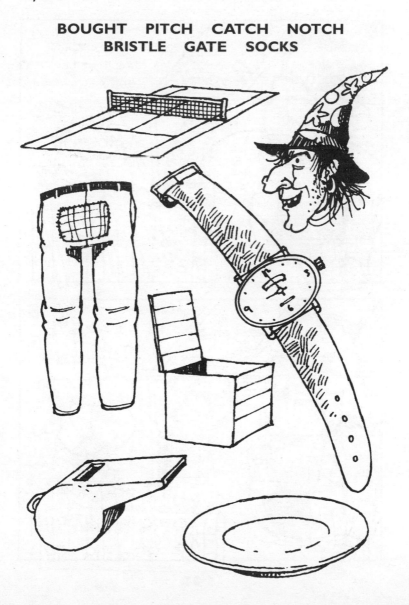

Own Goal!

Which two pictures of this unfortunate footballer are exactly the same?

Home Grounds

Match the teams on the left with their home grounds on the right.

1	Manchester United	St Andrews
2	Juventus	Molineux
3	Arsenal	Anfield Road
4	Barcelona	Loftus Road
5	Marseille	Stamford Bridge
6	Liverpool	Old Trafford
7	Rangers	Emirates Stadium
8	Everton	Hillsborough
9	Wolverhampton Wanderers	Delle Alpi
10	Stirling Albion	Vélodrome
11	Chelsea	Ibrox Park
12	Coventry City	Non Camp
13	Birmingham City	Goodison Park
14	Queen's Park Rangers	Annfield Park
15	Sheffield Wednesday	Highfield Road

Cup Fever

Do you recognize these famous football trophies?

1.

2.

3.

4.

Pitching In

How much do you know about the pitch on which you play your favourite game?

1 What's the diameter of the centre circle?

2 What's the minimum height of the corner flag above the ground?

3 What are the dimensions of the goal?

4 Are goalposts square or round in section?

5 What's the name of this rectangle?

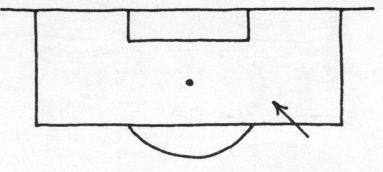

6 Can a soccer field be more than 130 yards long?

Team Badges I

Can you identify these six British team badges?

1.

2.

3.

4.

5.

6.

Cryptic Crossword

This puzzle is strictly for crossword addicts, as it has a number of cryptic clues, just like an adult crossword. The key is to work them out bit by bit.

Across

1 Twelve inches, Queen Elizabeth – gives slang name for your favourite sport (6)
4 Ten and one gives a team (6)
7 Al gets left – and everyone (3)
8 United Nations keeps things in order – disorderly (6)
10 Northern British city ends with sandwich filling (6)
12 South, north or tea, initially, makes a horse noise (5)
15 Ajax Amsterdam player is this (5)
17 He or she has possession (5)
19 Belonging to Roman X, frequently (5)
20 Restore – regarding something just made (5)
22 Speak quietly without mother at the beginning – also means speak (5)
25 Scottish rap gives a small piece (5)
28 Speedy, east, north – do up buttons (6)
29 Hit with top part of body – into net? (6)
30 Number one card – very clever! (3)
31 Famous Parisian tower (6)
32 Change direction (6)

Down

1 Dirtied – or played on fairly (6)
3 Sun's beam, on – gives a kind of fabric (5)
4 Kind of tree is older (5)
6 Six is one, so is one (6)
9 Person who sells tickets – often at high prices (4)
11 It may be sung in church or at a match (4)
12 Demonstrates (5)
13 Not inner (5)

14 Heavy weight above – describes someone who rides a motorbike at over 100 mph (3-2)

16 America, east, means employ (3)

18 Keep it on the ball! (3)

20 Type of ticket you buy hoping to win something (6)

21 Goals have them, fish avoid them (4)

23 Scored equally (4)

24 Conundrum (see next page?) (6)

26 Can Al sail a boat on it? (5)

27 Gives pain (your legs may do this after too much football!) (5)

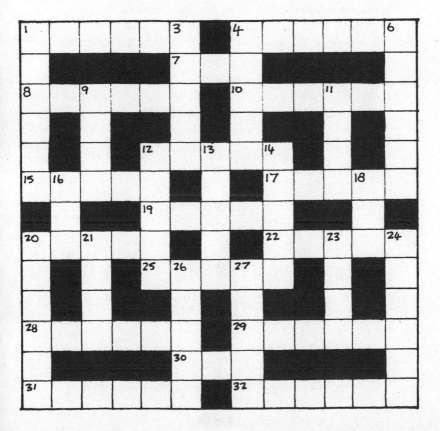

Riddle-me-ree

Solve the riddle.

My first is in tackle but never in shoot,
My second's in dribble but never in boot.
My third is in volley and also in view,
My fourth's in the centre of ref and of new.
My fifth is in Rangers and also Montrose,
My sixth is in practice, professional and prose.
My seventh whole letter is round, like a ball,
My eighth is the same, as wide as it's tall.
My ninth's in pullover, but never in jersey,
My whole is a team that plays on the Mersey.

Right and Left

How many right and how many left football boots can you spot in the picture? Note that the stripes are on the outside of the boots.

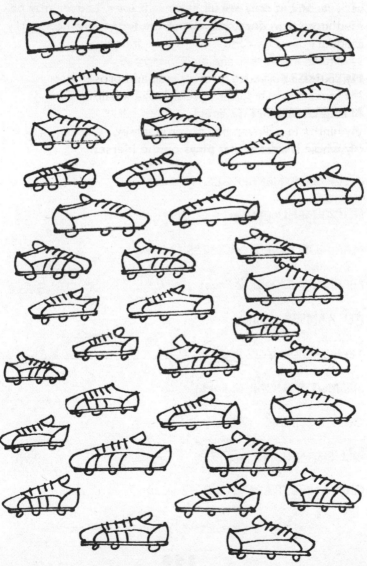

Great Names

The names of all the famous coaches and managers listed below can be found in the grid. The words may read across, up, down or diagonally, either forwards or backwards, but they are all in straight lines. Letters may be used more than once, but not all the letters are necessarily used.

MATT BUSBY

ALEX FERGUSON (2 lines)

HELENIO HERRERA (2 lines)

JOSEF 'SEPP' HERBERGER (3 lines)

HUGO MEISL (2 lines)

MARINUS 'RINUS' MICHELS (2 lines)

FERENC PUSKAS (2 lines)

ALF RAMSEY (2 lines)

TELE SANTANA (2 lines)

HELMUT SCHON (2 lines)

GUSZTAV SEBES (2 lines)

BILL SHANKLY (2 lines)

GIOVANNI TRAPATTONI (2 lines)

M	A	T	T	B	U	S	B	Y	N	M	F	G
I	A	T	L	S	I	E	M	L	P	R	E	O
C	N	R	L	S	K	B	T	K	R	E	R	I
H	H	G	I	N	Q	E	L	N	A	G	G	N
E	E	U	B	N	L	S	C	A	M	R	U	E
L	R	S	G	E	U	N	N	H	S	E	S	L
S	R	Z	I	O	D	S	E	S	B	O	E	
A	E	T	O	F	M	E	R	D	Y	R	N	H
K	R	A	V	E	K	P	E	I	L	E	O	E
S	A	V	A	S	Q	P	F	G	N	H	H	L
U	B	L	N	O	B	D	L	V	W	U	C	M
P	E	J	N	J	A	N	A	T	N	A	S	U
X	W	N	I	N	O	T	T	A	P	A	R	T

What's Wrong?

Our artist doesn't know much about football! How many mistakes has he made in this picture?

Jeremiah doesn't know much about football. How many
mistakes can you spot in this football scene? Is out of all the
players mixed up, and who's doing what, and where the ball is,
and what everyone else is doing and all the other things.

O Tired Dun Fox!

The heading of this page is an anagram of a British football team, that is, a rearrangement of the letters to spell out different words. Can you spot which team it is? And when you've done so, can you work out what all the teams below are? (NB They're all British.)

1   TRACY SCALP ALE.

2   I.E. ONE MUST RUSH.

3   FED, SHE SAID, DENY FLEW.

4   BAN HIM, GRIM.

5   QUEUE, THEN HOOF ST.

6   DIG ELM SHRUB, DO.

7   FROM HOT SENT GIANT.

8   TUM SHOP ROT.

9   TRY ICY OVEN, T.C.

10   MULE INN, FRED.

11   TRAM HERO, H.

12   FRIED ETCH, LES.

True or False? 1

Are the following statements true or false?

1 You cannot score a goal from a direct free kick.

2 The referee's signal for an indirect free kick is to hold his left arm up in the air.

3 Aluminium studs in football boots are useful on wet, slippery ground.

4 A volley is a pass made by kicking the ball when it's on the ground.

5 You are allowed to stop the ball with your chest provided you don't touch it with your hands or arms.

6 Sol Campbell once played for Tottenham Hotspur.

7 David Beckham supported Arsenal as a kid.

True or False? II

Are the following statements true or false?

1 Celtic's home ground is Ibrox Park.

2 Ryan Giggs's first international match appearance was for Wales in 1991.

3 Manchester United fans have a song about Ryan Giggs which is sung to the tune of 'Popeye the Sailorman'.

4 Frank Lampard's dad was a professional footballer.

5 Andrei Shevchenko is Polish.

6 Wayne Rooney was born in Manchester.

7 You use an overarm throw to throw a ball a long distance and an underarm throw to throw it a short distance.

Spot the Ball

This drawing is based on a real-life photograph, but the ball has been omitted from it. Can you spot where it is?

In the Locker Room

This puzzle is an acrostic. If you solve the clues correctly and fill in the answers in the grid you will find, reading down the arrowed column, something else you might see in the locker room, especially if you're a fan of Chelsea, Sheffield Wednesday or Chesterfield!

1 They're worn on the feet (5)

2 They're used to fasten no.1 (5)

3 Players wear one on their backs (6)

4 A goalkeeper wears one of these (6)

5 You might wear one of these for training (5, 4)

6, 7 You wear these under your socks (4, 4)

8 If there's a shower, you'll need one of these (5)

9 Footwear (5)

10 The top half of your strip (5)

11 The lower half of your strip (6)

12 Goalkeepers wear these (6)

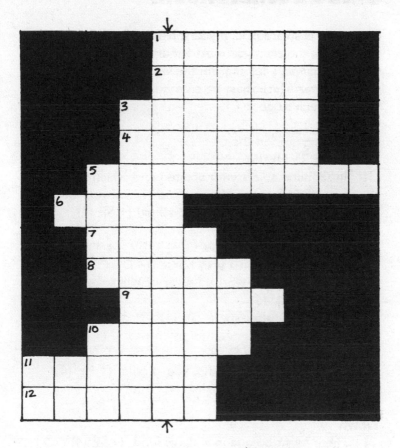

Plus or Minus?

This is a crossword puzzle with a difference. When you have solved the clue, you must either *add* a letter to the word or *subtract* a letter from the word in order to arrive at the answer which must be entered in the grid. The clues tell you which to do.

Across

1 Broad (+ N) (5)
4 Small metal object with pointed end which holds pieces of fabric together, or with which you can fasten a brooch or badge to your clothes (+ S) (4)
6 Fear (– F) (5)
7 A letter might end 'Yours, _ _ _ _ ' (+ Y) (5)
9 Round marking on a grey horse (– D) (5)
12 Defending player who stays very close to attacking player (– R) (5)
14 The number after six (– S) (4)
15 All the things you need to play football (+ E) (4)
18 Further down (+ S) (6)
20 You _ _ _ _ _ to do this, you should (+ B) (6)
21 Joint at the top of your leg (+ C) (4)

Down

1 There might be one in a playground (– S) (4)
2 It's in the middle of your face (+ I) (5)
3 It might catch a mouse (+ S) (5)
4 Eleven players form one (+ S) (5)
5 This chicken's a great _ _ _ _ _ (+ P) (6)
8 Long for (– E) (4)
10 Creep along quietly in the shadows (– S) (4)
11 Positioned in the middle (– D) (6)
13 Ability (– S) (4)
16 Male deer (– S) (3)
17 The best team is top of the league _ _ _ _ _ (– T) (4)

18 The opposite of 'bottom' (+ S) (4)
19 Alcoholic drink made from grapes (– E) (3)

Your Number's Up!

How good is your maths? Test it with these taxing problems.

1   How can a boy carry nine footballs in four bags and have an odd number in each bag?

2   Ryan is twice as old as Brian. When Ryan was four times as old as Brian, Brian was just three. How old are Ryan and Brian?

3   Daniel had been saving up 1p, 2p and 5p coins in his piggy bank for many weeks. One day he decided he must now be rich enough to buy a football book that cost £3.99, so he opened the pigggy bank and poured the coins out on to the table. There were 30 1p coins, 43 2p coins and 17 5p coins. Did he have enough money to buy the football book, and if not, how much more did he need?

4   In the school sports day football tournament there were five teams – A, B, C, D and E. C finished in front of D but behind A. E finished in front of B but behind D. In which order did they finish the tournament?

In the Negative

Which of the pictures below is the one shown in the negative above?

Goal Tally

How many times can you find the word BALL in the grid below; and how many times can you find the word GOAL in the grid opposite? Count carefully – there may be more than you think! The words may read across, up, down or diagonally, either forwards or backwards. They are all in straight lines. Each letter in the grid may be used more than once, but not all of them are necessarily used. Use a pencil and a ruler to cross out the words as you find them.

B	L	A	B	A	L	L	A	B
A	A	B	A	L	L	B	A	A
L	L	L	L	B	L	L	B	L
L	L	L	L	L	L	L	A	L
A	A	A	A	L	L	L	L	A
B	B	B	B	B	A	A	L	B
A	A	A	A	A	B	B	L	A
L	L	L	L	L	L	A	A	L
L	L	L	L	L	A	L	B	L

G	L	O	A	G	O	A	L	A	O	G
O	O	A	L	A	O	G	O	G	O	O
A	A	A	O	G	A	A	O	A	L	A
L	G	G	L	G	L	A	L	A	A	L
A	G	O	A	L	L	G	O	A	L	A
O	A	A	A	G	G	G	O	A	L	O
G	O	L	O	L	O	L	A	A	A	G
O	L	A	O	A	A	A	O	L	O	O
A	L	L	L	O	L	G	L	A	G	A
L	A	A	A	G	O	A	L	O	O	L
O	O	O	O	L	O	A	O	G	A	A
G	G	G	G	O	A	A	G	G	L	O
A	L	A	O	G	O	A	L	A	O	G

Grandstand

How many differences can you spot between these two pictures of a grandstand?

Word Chain

Solve the clues and fill in the letters clockwise in this grid, in which the last letter of one word is the first letter of the one following it.

1 A goalkeeper may bring the ball back into play with this (4)
2 The goal should be your _ _ _ _ _ (6)
3 The team may work these out before a match (7)
4 The goalie's job is to stop people doing this (7)
5 You may be able to slide in one of these near the goal (6, 4)
6 You may use this to bring a dead ball back into play (5-2)
7 The goal is covered by this (7)

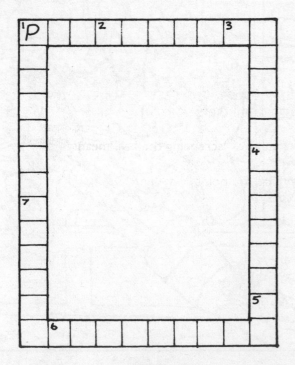

Technical Stuff

1 With what part of your foot do you kick the ball when making a push pass?

2 With which part of your foot do you kick the ball when making a flick pass?

3 What's another name for a banana shot?

4 If you are trying to intercept a ball heading towards you how do you stop it bouncing off your foot?

5 What is 'trapping'?

6 In a side block tackle, do you drag or kick the ball away from your opponent?

7 What are the 'in-swinger' and the 'out-swinger' types of?

8 If you are about to throw in the ball, where do you hold it and throw it from?

9 What does 'screening the ball' mean?

10 What's the point of a chip shot?

Where?

1 Where is the ball placed for the kick-off?

2 If the opposite side is taking a corner kick and the penalty area is crowded, where should the goalkeeper stand?

3 At the kick-off, where should the players be?

4 Where is the Azteca Stadium?

5 Where is the San Paulo Stadium?

6 Which club was Alan Shearer with before Newcastle United?

7 Where can you put an optional flagstaff?

8 Where was the first World Cup Final held in 1930?

9 With which Midlands town was Stanley Matthews associated?

10 Which club did David Beckham leave Manchester United for?

Team Badges II

Can you identify these European team badges?

1

2

3

4

5

6

Ref's Reference

Could you be a ref? See how much you know about the rules of your favourite game.

1 Can a referee caution a player before the game has started if that player and the referee are on the pitch?

2 What should a referee do if a player appears to be badly hurt?

3 If an incident has occurred in which a free kick would give an advantage to the team in the wrong, what should the referee do?

4 Has the referee the power to prevent people other than the players and linesmen from entering the pitch?

5 What does a referee note on his record card? See how many of the ten things in the answer you can name.

6 What kind of watch should a referee wear?

7 Why are red and yellow cards different shapes?

8 What colours should linesmen's flags be, and who provides them?

9 Can a player be cautioned if he disagrees with the referee's decision?

10 How should the referee hold a red or yellow card?

11 If a player commits a misconduct during the half-time interval, can the referee take action against him?

All Square

Which three squares of this squared-up picture are exactly the same?

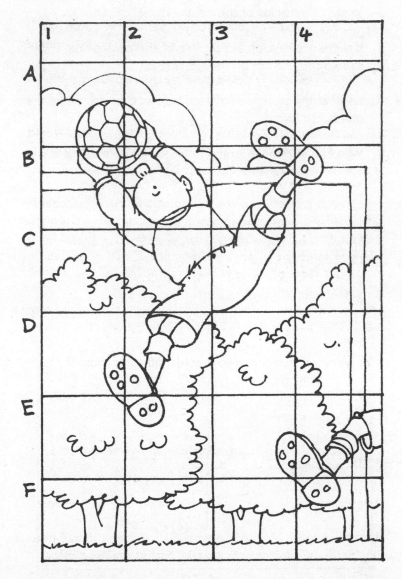

On the Ground

1 What's the minimum width of a soccer pitch?

2 What's the radius of the centre circle?

3 If there are flags on either side of the centre line, should they be set on the touchline?

4 Look at the picture of a pitch below. Can you name the numbered parts?

5 What should the distance be between points A and B? Should it be 22 yards (20.1m), 25 yards (22.8m) or 30 yards (27.4m)?

6 What should the distance be between points C and D? Should it be 2 feet (0.6m), 3 feet (0.9m) or 4 feet (1.21m)?

7 What's the 'six-yard box' also known as?

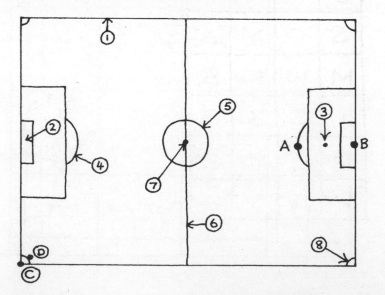

Cup Final Grid

Hidden in each of these grids are two names connected with the 1997 FA Cup Final. Can you spot what they are?

	A	E
E	L	S
H	I	L
C	T	L
U	U	U
R	D	G

B	O	R	N
S	O	Y	A
M	N	R	B
I	S	B	H
D	E	R	G
D	L	O	U

Great Save!

Which of these pictures is the odd one out, and why?

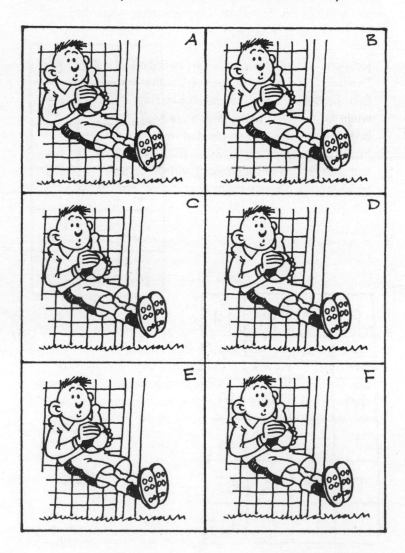

Baffling Brainteasers

1 What's the next number in the series?

11 1 12 1 1 1 2 1 3 1

2 John and Jim are, respectively, Sheffield United and Sheffield Wednesday supporters. One Saturday John's father is taking him to an away match in Manchester, while Jim's dad is taking Jim to an away match in Birmingham. If John and his dad must travel 38 miles to Manchester, and they drive at 40 mph, and Jim and his dad must travel 76 miles to Birmingham and they drive at 50 mph, who gets there first if they both leave at 11 a.m.?

3 If you go to bed at 7.30 on the night the clocks are put forward for British Summer Time, having set your alarm clock to wake you up at 8.30 for football practice the next morning, how much sleep will you get?

4 You want to buy some new football boots and your mum and dad say you must save up for them. If you save 1p the first day, 2p the second day, 4p the third day, 8p the fourth, and so on, saving twice as much each day as you saved the day before, how long will it take you to save enough for the boots if they cost £20?

Missing Lines

Some of the straight lines have disappeared, but can you read the message?

MY TEAM

WILL WIN

IN THE

FINAL

Answers

Page 101 Rules of the Game

1 Eleven. **2** The goalkeeper. **3** Players other than the goalkeeper may move the ball with any part of their body except the hands or arms. **4** Two. **5** With flags. **6** Three (in British football). **7** 45 minutes. **8** Fifteen minutes. **9** The whole of the ball must cross the goal line under the crossbar and between the posts. **10** No. It must cross the touchline completely to be out of play. **11** One from which a goal cannot be scored until the ball has been touched by another player. **12** At least 10 yards (9.14 m) away. **13** At the start of the game it should weigh 14–16 oz (397–454 g). **14** Clothes that are a different colour from those worn by the rest of the players and the referee. **15** Only with the referee's permission.

Page 102 Afternoon Out

1 45 sweets. **2** 32,500. **3** £1.15.

Page 103 Woolly Mufflers

There are 19 football scarves in the picture.

Page 104 Picture Puzzle

Page 106 First Half

There are 10 differences between the pictures.

Page 108 Name-dropping
1 Vinnie Jones. 2 Marco Tardelli. 3 Jurgen Klinsmann.
4 Bobby Charlton. 5 Jean-Pierre Papin. 6 Diego
Maradona. 7 Paul Gascoigne. 8 Kenny Dalglish.
9 Johan Cruyff. 10 Roberto Baggio.
11 Eric Cantona. 12 Gary Lineker.

Page 109 Cup Tie
Picture letter D.

Page 110 Free Kick

The left-over letters spell out FIRST DIVISION.

Page 112 Who?
1 Kenny Dalglish. 2 Pele. 3 Eusebio. 4 Diego
Maradona. 5 Johan Cruyff. 6 Billy Wright. 7 Bobby
Moore. 8 Stephen Gerrard. 9 Real Madrid.
10 Everton.

Page 113 On the Line
1 Goal kick. 2 Advise awarding penalty kick.
3 Substitution. 4 Corner kick.

Page 114 Odd One Out

1 Bramall Lane: it is in Sheffield; the other two are in Glasgow.   2 Trapping: it is the art of bringing high or bouncing balls under control; the other two are types of tackle.   3 Juventus: it is an Italian team; the others are Russian.   4 Nacional: it is a team from Uruguay; the others are Brazilian.   5 Link-man: he is a midfield player; the others are forwards.   6 Dribble: it is moving the ball along; the others are shots.   7 Out-swinger: it is a corner kick; the others are goalkeeper's throws.   8 Heading: the others are fouls.   9 Forward short leg: it is a cricket position; the others are football positions.   10 Rose Bowl: it is an American Football trophy; the others are soccer trophies.

Page 115 Knotty Problem

Laces A belong to boot 2 ; laces B to boot 3 ; laces C to boot 1.

Page 116 What's in a Name?

1 When the attacker has fewer than two opposing players between him and the goal at the time the ball was played.
2 A kick given as compensation for a foul. It may be direct or indirect.   3 One of a number of offences committed intentionally by a player on his opponent while the ball is in play, such as kicking him, tripping him up, charging at him, holding him, pushing him, and so on.
4 A kick awarded in the penalty area to the attacking side if the defending side have committed one of nine penal offences.   5 If the ball crosses completely over the touchline, this is awarded by the referee to the opposite team of the player who last played it.   6 A card the referee holds up when cautioning a player.   7 A card the referee holds up when sending off a player.   8 Flicking the ball forward or sideways with the outside of the foot.
9 Cutting the foot across the inside or outside of the ball

to make it 'bend'.   **10** Kicking the ball immediately after it bounces.   **11** Saving the ball by flinging yourself towards it and ending up on the ground.   **12** Deflecting the ball from entering the goal by hitting it with a clenched fist.

Page 117 What's Missing?
A Stripe on sleeve.   **B** Lock.   **C** Peg
D Contents of bag.   **E** Laces.

Page 118 Gridlock
1l.   3D.   5G.   7A.   9C.   11G.   13B.   15G.

Page 120 Getting Fit
The arrowed column spells out RYAN GIGGS.

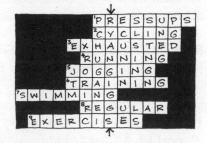

Page 122 Field of Play
1 Outside left.   **2 and 3** Centre forwards (strikers).
4 Outside right.   **5 and 6** Link-men.   **7** Left back.
8 and 9 Centre halves.   **10** Right back.
11 Goalkeeper.

Page 123 Fill the Gaps
1 Leeds United.   **2** Wimbledon.   **3** Charlton Athletic.
4 Chelsea.   **5** Manchester United.
6 Tottenham Hotspur.   **7** Aston Villa.   **8** Bristol
Rovers.   **9** Preston North End.   **10** Partick Thistle.
11 Derby County.   **12** Wolverhampton Wanderers.

Page 124 Odd Picture Out
Picture C is the odd one out because grandstand roof is lower.

Page 126 Make It Fit

Page 128 Nicknames

1 York City. 2 Sheffield United. 3 Aston Villa.
4 West Ham United. 5 Chelsea. 6 Stoke City.
7 Arsenal. 8 Swansea City. 9 Derby County.
10 Scunthorpe United. 11 Reading. 12 Celtic.
13 Dundee United. 14 Millwall. 15 Mansfield Town.

Page 129 How Many?

There are 8 patterns on the footballs.

Page 130 Word Snake

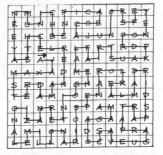

Page 132 Hidden in a Sentence

1 Captain. 2 Defence. 3 Forward. 4 Field.
5 Pitch. 6 Offside. 7 Save. 8 Ball. 9 Team.
10 Corner.

Page 133 Striking

Striker C.

Page 134 Observation Test

1 The player at the bottom right is doing the press-ups.
2 The curly-haired player is lifting weights. **3** Player
number 5. **4** Four players. **5** Black shorts and striped
shirts. **6** A tracksuit with stripes down the sides of the
legs. **7** His left hand. **8** There are 3 trees in the
background. **9** Three cows. **10** Two. **11** Player
number 7.

Page 136 Header!
There are 9 differences.

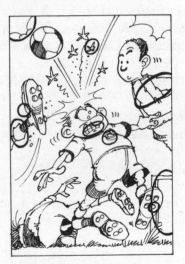

Page 138 Buying Kit
Buy a shirt, shorts and socks (£53.97); then either boots
(**b**) and football (**a**) (£87.95); or boots (**a**) and football
(**c**) (£89.95).

Page 139 Rhyme Time
BOUGHT and court (tennis court); PITCH and witch;
CATCH and patch (on trousers); NOTCH and watch;
BRISTLE and whistle; GATE and plate; SOCKS and box.

Page 140 Own Goal!
Pictures B and C are exactly the same.

Page 142 Home Grounds
1 Old Trafford.   2 Delle Alpi.   3 Emirates Stadium.
4 Non Camp.   5 Vélodrome.   6 Anfield Road.
7 Ibrox Park.   8 Goodison Park.   9 Molineux.
10 Annfield Park.   11 Stamford Bridge.   12 Highfield
Road.   13 St Andrews.   14 Loftus Road.
15 Hillsborough.

Page 143 Cup Fever
1 European Cup.   2 World Cup.   3 European
Championship Trophy.   4 European Cup-winners' Cup.

Page 144 Pitching In
1 20 yards (18.3 m).   2 5 feet (1.52 m)   3 8 feet
(2.44 m) high by 24 feet (7.32 m) wide.   4 Either.
5 The penalty area.   6 No, it must be between 100 and
130 yards long (91–119 m).

Page 145 Team Badges 1
1 Everton.   2 Arsenal.   3 Chelsea.   4 Nottingham
Forest.   5 Raith Rovers.   6 Leicester City.

**Page 146 Cryptic
Crossword**

Page 148 Riddle-me-ree

L - I - V - E - R - P - O - O - L

Page 149 Right and Left

There are 21 right and 15 left boots in the picture.

Page 150
Great Names

Page 152 What's Wrong?

The following things are wrong: goalie wearing same clothes as other players, player holding ball, two balls in play, rugby posts, goal netting wrong, sleeping player, dog on pitch, incorrect markings on pitch.

Page 154 O Tired Dun Fox!*

1 Crystal Palace. **2** Stenhousemuir. **3** Sheffield Wednesday. **4** Birmingham. **5** Queen of the South.
6 Middlesbrough. **7** Nottingham Forest.
8 Portsmouth. **9** Coventry City. **10** Dunfermline.
11 Rotherham. **12** Chesterfield.
* The heading is an anagram of Oxford United.

Page 155 True or False? I

1 False; you can. **2** True. **3** True. **4** False; it's a pass made by kicking it when it is in the air. **5** True.
6 True. **7** False; he has always supported Manchester United.

Page 156 True or False? II

1 False; Ibrox Park is Rangers' home ground. **2** True.

186

3 True. **4** False; he is Russian. **5** False; he is Romanian. **6** False; Liverpool. **7** True.

Page 157
Spot the Ball

Page 158 In the
Locker Room

The arrowed column spells out BLUE AND WHITE.

Page 160
Plus or Minus?

Page 162 Your Number's Up!

1 He puts three footballs in each of three bags and then puts the three bags into a fourth, larger, bag. **2** Ryan is 18 and Brian is nine. **3** He had saved £2.01 so he still needed another £1.98 to buy the book. **4** A was first, followed by C, D, E and B.

Page 163 In the Negative

Footballer A.

Page 164 Goal Tally

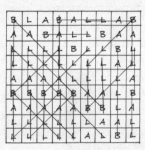 

The word BALL appears in the smaller grid 34 times; the word GOAL in the larger grid 42 times.

Page 166 Grandstand

There are 10 differences.

Page 168 Word Chain

```
P U N T A R G E T A
G                 C
N                 T
I                 I
T                 C
T                 S
E                 C
N                 O
I                 R
W                 I
O                 N
R                 G
H T O H S D N U O R
```

Page 169 Technical Stuff

1 The inside.   2 The outside.   3 'Bending' the ball.
4 By keeping your foot as relaxed as possible.   5 The art of bringing high or bouncing balls under control instantly.
6 Drag it.   7 Corner kick.   8 Behind and over your head.   9 Shielding it from an opponent with your body.
10 To lift the ball over a short distance.

Page 170 Where?

1 On the centre spot in the middle of the centre circle.
2 Near the centre of the goal.   3 Every player should be in his own half.   4 Mexico City.   5 Naples.
6 Blackburn Rovers.   7 At either end of the halfway line.
8 Centenario Stadium, Montevideo, Uruguay.
9 Stoke-on-Trent.   10 Real Madrid.

Page 171 Team Badges II

1 Moscow Dynamo.   2 Milan.   3 Go Ahead Eagles (Holland).   4 FC Bayern München.   5 Valencia.
6 Lille OSC (France).

Page 172 Ref's Reference

1 Yes.   2 Stop the game.   3 Not allow the free kick.
4 Yes.   5 The date, team names and colours, the captains' numbers, the kick-off times, the score, details of cautions and dismissals, substitutes, and the linesmen's names.   6 A stopwatch.   7 So the referee can tell

which is which when the cards are still in his pocket to avoid pulling out the wrong one by mistake.   **8** Bright colours. They are provided by the home team.   **9**   Yes.
10   High up in the air with his arm held vertically.
11 Yes.

Page 173 All Square
Squares A3. D1. and E3 are identical.

Page 174 On the Ground
1 50 yards (45.7 m).   **2** 10 yards (9.1 m).   **3** No, they must be set back at least 1 yard (0.9 m) from the touchline.
4 1) Touchline. 2) Goal area. 3) Penalty mark.
4) Penalty arc. 5) Centre circle. 6) Halfway line.
7) Centre mark. 8) Corner area.   **5** 22 yards (20.1 m)
6 3 feet (0.9 m).   **7** The goal area.

Page 175 Cup Final Grid
The hidden names are
RUUD GULLIT, CHELSEA
and BRYAN ROBSON
MIDDLESBROUGH

Page 176 Great Save!
Picture D is the odd one out.
Because the goal net is complete beneath his left hand.

Page 177 Baffling Brainteasers
1 4. They are the sequence of chimes of a chiming clock that strikes the hours and half hours, starting with 11 o'clock.   **2** John and his dad arrive first at 11.57 a.m.; Jim and his dad arrive at 12.31.   **3** One hour. Unless you have a 24-hour clock, the alarm will go off at 8.30 p.m. the same night.   **4** Eleven days.

Page 178 Missing Lines
The message reads: MY TEAM WILL WIN IN THE FINAL.

FOOTBALL CROSSWORDS

by Roy and Sue Preston

No 1

ACROSS

2 People who discover new players, talent ____ (6).
6 Bird linked with the nickname of Crystal Palace (5).
7 The deciding game in a knockout competition (5).
9 French superstar Cantona (4).
10 Relegation means a team goes in this direction (4).
12 Part of the pitch, the penalty (4).
15 Joint in the leg (4).
18 Number of goals in a hat-trick (5).
19 Another word for a soccer game (5).
20 Plot and plan (6).

DOWN

1 Man Utd's home, Old ____ (8).
3 Football team from Stamford Bridge (7).
4 Welsh veteran Garry of Bolton, Newcastle, Everton and Leeds (5).
5 Scottish legend Mr Dalglish (5).
8 A bad sport who tells untruths (4).
11 Edge of the pitch or part of a bird (4).
13 Describes someone who is fit. Oldham and Charlton share this name (8).
14 London club whose supporters sing about 'blowing bubbles' (4,3).
16 Birmingham's much-travelled striker Sutton (5).
17 Man City's keeper David (5).

195

No 2

ACROSS

2 Number on the scoreboard when the score is nil (6).

6 Champions finish in this place in the Premiership (5).

7 Knocks the ball with the foot (5).

9 A goalie wants to catch a high ball, he does not want to _____ it (4).

10 Attempt at goal (4).

12 Ipswich ground, Portman _____ (4).

15 Express disapproval verbally (4).

18 Moves round, spins (5).

19 Two wins and two draws in the Premiership gets how many points? (5).

20 Road where Leeds play (6).

DOWN

1 A goalkeeper cannot pick this up from a team-mate (4,4).

3 An attacker is this when he moves too early beyond the last defender (7).

4 A championship (5).

5 Foot and lower leg coverings (5).

8 In short, Middlesbrough's nickname (4).

11 A goal is this if it's unguarded (4).

13 Promotion means your team moves up a _____ (8).

14 Famous Park which is Portsmouth's home (7).

16 Put the ball back in play with hands not feet (5).

17 Manager Mr Coppell (5).

197

No 3

ACROSS

2 Freddie Ljunberg's country (6).
6 Team from Milan (5).
7 Beastly nickname for Millwall (5).
9 Take this when a side goes ahead (4).
10 Legendary Brazilian star of the 50s, 60s and 70s (4).
12 Use this to meet a high ball (4).
15 Man Utd's French striker Louis (4).
18 Mr Beckham (5).
19 Aston _____ (4).
20 Bolton striker Kevin (6).

DOWN

1 Global soccer tournament held every four years (5,3).
3 Blown by a referee (7).
4 Preston _____ End (5).
5 Ball from the wings into the penalty area (5).
8 White Hart _____ (4).
11 Jump high for a header (4).
13 Ground home to 4 down (8).
14 Protective cover for a wound (7).
16 Name for a dog who supports Blackburn? (5).
17 Kept out by the keeper (5).

No 4

ACROSS

2 People who represent players (6).
6 Manager of the Month ___ (5).
7 White markings around a pitch (5).
9 England star striker Michael (4).
10 Manager Adams, a former Arsenal legend (5).
12 Prepare material for a programme (4).
15 Fixture (4).
18 WBA boss Robson (5).
19 Month when F.A. Cup semifinals are played (5).
20 Everton's veteran keeper Nigel (6).

DOWN

1 Upright of the target area on a pitch (4,4).
3 City with Rangers and Celtic (7).
4 Teams (5).
5 French star Thierry (5).
8 Curl a free-kick and ___ it like Beckham (4).
11 This sort of miss is only just wide (4).
13 Skilled, gifted (8).
14 Home stadium for England (7).
16 Scottish team known as The Bully Wee (5).
17 Appeal or shout for a penalty (5).

NO 5

ACROSS

2 Rotherham, Torquay and West Ham are all this (6).

6 Chelsea billionaire Mr Abramovich (5).

7 Give a disputed goal (5).

9 It can be yellow. It can be red (4).

10 At half-time teams change _____ (4).

12 The Scottish F.A. Cup Final is played once a _____ (4).

15 Man Utd's Ji-Sung _____ (4).

18 Man Utd's famous former keeper Schmeichel (5).

19 Lively and quick thinking (5).

20 Arsenal ace Pires (6).

DOWN

1 Draw level (8).

3 Team from Norfolk (7).

4 Man City defender Richard (5).

5 Gillingham's nickname (5).

8 A transfer costing no money (4).

11 Transfer that goes ahead (4).

13 Match officials (8).

14 Another name for captain (7).

16 Grab the ball with the hands (5).

17 Not a winner (5).

No 6

ACROSS

2 Leicester's former ground Filbert _____ (6).
6 Spectators (5).
7 England midfielder Lampard (5).
9 A game does this when it finishes (4).
10 Animal nickname for Derby County (4).
12 Applaud (4).
15 Mr Mourinho (4).
18 Player who goes to ground too easily (5).
19 Hymn linked with the F.A. Cup Final. '_____ with me' (5).
20 Notts team not County (6).

DOWN

1 Burnley's home (4,4).
3 Challenges for the ball (7).
4 West Ham's veteran striker Sheringham (5).
5 David Beckham moved to play in this country when he left Man Utd (5).
8 Hero (4).
11 Really happy, over the _____ (4).
13 Blackburn winger Morten (8).
14 Team at the top (7).
16 Take the place of someone out of position (5).
17 Worn round the neck by a fan (5).

No 7

ACROSS

2 Villa keeper Sorensen (6).
6 Blackburn's Turkish midfielder (5).
7 Only player to score a World Cup Final hat trick, England's Geoff ____ (5).
9 A quick break forward (4).
10 Ipswich ____ (4).
12 Ref needs these in the back of his head (4).
15 Red flower featured on Blackburn's emblem (4).
18 Written tests, as taken on coaching courses (5).
19 Change the way the team are playing, ____ tactics (5).
20 Touch the ball but not with the foot (6).

DOWN

1 Crystal Palace ground ____ Park (8).
3 Luton's mad nickname (7).
4 Class (5).
5 Liverpool forward Kewell (5).
8 Cardiff, Leicester and Stoke share this name (4).
11 Hit the goal-post, hit the ____ work (4).
13 Move quickly to evade a tackle (8)
14 Person who starts a match (7).
16 Country with Real Madrid and Barcelona (5).
17 Train and develop the players (5).

No 8

ACROSS

2 Play in another country, go —— (6).

6 Command, as in leave the field (5).

7 Subtle touch (5).

9 Traditional shirt number of a centre-forward (4).

10 Walk with difficulty (4).

12 Caught (4).

15 Result earning one point (4).

18 Man Utd keeper Van der Saar (5).

19 Run of poor form (5).

20 Man City boss Mr Pearce (6).

DOWN

1 Last game in a knock-out competition (3,5).

3 Yellow card means this (7).

4 Match between near neighbours (5).

5 Cold-sounding South American country that hosted the 1962 World Cup (5).

8 Footballer's cartilage problem often affects this joint (4).

11 Australian striker Viduka (4).

13 Player protecting the goal (8).

14 Defender who cleans up behind others (7).

16 Crystal Palace boss Iain (5).

17 Goal supports (5).

No 9

ACROSS

2 World Cup winners in 2002 (6).

6 Birmingham midfielder _____ Butt (5).

7 Wayne Rooney was voted 2005 _____ Player of the Year (5).

9 Welsh wizard _____ Giggs (4).

10 Crowd call when a team is walking over the opposition (4).

12 Liverpool or Man Utd colour nickname (4).

15 On target . . . on the _____ (4).

18 Place for a sub to sit (5).

19 Personal award made to winning players (5).

20 Number of players in a side (6).

DOWN

1 Man City's veteran much-travelled striker (4,4).

3 Club from Ibrox (7).

4 Colchester home, _____ Road (5).

5 In short, it's Tottenham (5).

8 A ref may take this (4).

11 Mark left on the skin after a cut (4).

13 Essex club from Root's Hall (8).

14 Coventry colour (3,4).

16 An outfield player cannot use these (5).

17 Liverpool defender Carragher (5).

No 10

ACROSS

2 Popular ref Mr _____ Poll (6).

6 Ability (5).

7 English skipper of 1966 World Cup winning team, Bobby _____ (5).

9 Port F.C. (4).

10 Opposite of away (4).

12 You can do this with a drum or with the opposition! (4).

15 Fancy-sounding nickname of Peterborough (4).

18 Bolton Midfielder Nolan (5).

19 Undo, as with a bootlace (5).

20 Nationality of Thomas Gravesen (6).

DOWN

1 Team with green and black strip from Home Park (8).

3 A player not in the first team (7).

4 Italian city with sides A.C. and Inter (5).

5 Didier Drogba's international team, _____ Coast (5).

8 Chelsea colour (4).

11 Show bad attitude, be in a bad _____ (4).

13 Practice and exercise get together (8).

14 Nickname for Bury (7).

16 Birmingham's midfielder Mr Dunn (5).

17 All the players at a club (5).

No 11

ACROSS

2 Type of free kick (6).

6 Newcastle midfielder Parker (5).

7 Restart play with a ____ in (5).

9 Lob or something to eat with a fish? (4).

10 Luton boss Mr Newell (4).

12 Side (4).

15 Player from north of the border (4).

18 Athletic team from a famous rugby town (5).

19 Time played *after* 90 minutes (5).

20 Fast moving (6).

DOWN

1 In short, the team from The Hawthorns (4,4).

3 E. Anglian side managed by Joe Royle (7).

4 Win this when you win a league (5).

5 Manager Redknapp (5).

8 Shown on TV as it happens (4).

11 Hit the ball (4).

13 Wolves' ground (8).

14 Person at a game helping crowd control (7).

16 Arsenal's French defender Pascal (5).

17 Newspapers, journalists and magazines – the ____ (5).

No 12

ACROSS

2 Charity trophy (6).
6 Red-breasted bird to find at Bristol City? (5).
7 Birmingham side Villa (5).
9 Offside snare (4).
10 Newcastle keeper ____ Given (4).
12 West Ham boss Pardew (4).
15 Liverpool's defender Hyppia (4).
18 Liverpool and England striker Crouch (5).
19 ____ Athletic, from the Recreation Park in Scotland (5).
20 Light a match or unleash a shot (6).

DOWN

1 Nickname of Norwich (8).
3 Nickname of Watford (7).
4 Charlton's midfielder Murphy (5).
5 Field of play (5).
8 Spurs and England keeper Robinson (4).
11 Not at home (4).
13 Nationality of Kanu and Babayaro (8).
14 Motherwell's ground (3,4).
16 Nationality of Dennis Bergkamp (5).
17 Waved by the linesmen (5).

No 13

ACROSS

2 Ask for a penalty (6).
6 Not left side or middle (5).
7 _____ of Midlothian (5).
9 Dropped (4).
10 Team from Crescent (4).
12 Supporters' association (4).
15 Reading striker Kitson (4).
18 Out of play, in _____ (5).
19 Running by Blackburn's ground, the _____ Darwen (5).
20 Bradford ground Valley _____ (6).

DOWN

1 Arsenal's stadium until 2006 (8).
3 Ipswich ground _____ Road (7).
4 Team from Kenilworth Road (5).
5 Nickname for Swansea (5).
8 Let a player leave for a fee (4).
11 QPR ground Loftus _____ (4).
13 South coast place to watch Seagulls (8).
14 Crossed from the wings (7).
16 Birmingham nickname (5).
17 Playing gear (5).

No 14

ACROSS

2 Dash at speed (6).

6 Corner of the upright and crossbar (5).

7 Pretend to leave the ball then leave it (5).

9 Man Utd ace Van Nistelrooy (4).

10 Wigan's ex-Liverpool striker _____ Mellor (4).

12 Famous player (4).

15 Brighton and _____ Albion (4).

18 Nationality of Roy Keane and Damian Duff (5).

19 Photographs of bones on an injured player (1,4).

20 Gerrard, or anyone from Liverpool (6).

DOWN

1 Everton's Park (8).

3 People on the park (7).

4 Layers in a stand that sound like they make you cry? (5).

5 Bolton's Spanish star Ivan (5).

8 Injured (4).

11 Use this to keep your kit without creases (4).

13 Player for Liverpool puts this on (3,5).

14 Holds on, defends in depth (7).

16 Scottish Rovers from Stark's Park (5).

17 Animal nickname of Leicester City? (5).

No 15

ACROSS

2 Man Utd and England star Wayne (6).

6 Last blow of the whistle (5).

7 Hit the net (5).

9 Shown by the referee (4).

10 Hurry (4).

12 Nickname for Sheffield Wednesday (4).

15 Grimsby, Halifax or Northampton (4).

18 Junior international side ____ 21's (5).

19 Roar on (5).

20 Quick (6).

DOWN

1 Horizontal goal pole (8).

3 Breaking of the rules. Soccer crime (7).

4 Shouts (5).

5 Keeper's hand gear (5).

8 The picking of teams to play against each other in a cup (4).

11 Penalty, a ____ kick (4).

13 Scottish team from St Mirren Park (2,6).

14 Hurt (7).

16 Teams (5).

17 Boot ties (5).

No 16

ACROSS

2 David Beckham has opened a soccer ——— for youngsters in London (6).

6 The goal is eight ____ wide (5).

7 Sprint-training command, 'On your ____, get set, go!' (5).

9 Lined section around the goal, the penalty ____ (4).

10 In short, it's Hibernian! (4).

12 Kick the ball with this (4).

15 Infringement (4).

18 Direct soccer, ____ one (5).

19 Club emblem on a shirt (5).

20 Beat soundly (6).

DOWN

1 Knockout game (3,5).

3 ____ Palace (7).

4 A game ____ for ninety minutes (5).

5 Position to aim for in a League (5).

8 Team idol (4).

11 Take a name, ____ someone (4).

13 Place for manager and subs to sit (3,5).

14 Burnley's colourful nickname (7).

16 Place to find teeth? Goal ____ (5).

17 First appearance (5).

No 17

ACROSS

2 Person who puts the ball in the net (6).

6 Opponent (5).

7 Popular Norwich keeper Robert (5).

9 Blackpool's ground, Bloomfield _____ (4).

10 Describes a capable keeper or a place to store money (4).

12 _____ Bromwich Albion (4).

15 City team from Humberside (4).

18 Fulham boss Mr Coleman (5).

19 A referee should _____ with a linesman if in doubt (5).

20 Places for spectators (6).

DOWN

1 Brighton birds (8).

3 Kicks from goal-line flags (7).

4 Tumbles over on the ground (5).

5 Manager Mr Hoddle (5).

8 F.A. non-league trophy or somewhere to put cut flowers (4).

11 Points gained by a Premiership win and a draw (4).

13 Move between clubs (8).

14 Stopped with the body (7).

16 French side _____ St Germain (5).

17 Touchline defenders (5).

No 18

ACROSS

2 Wrexham's home the Racecourse _____ (6).
6 Strength (5).
7 Level in score (5).
9 Henry and Lampard have been voted Footballer of the _____ (4).
10 At half-time teams change _____ (4).
12 Wing favoured by Kevin Kilbane and Ryan Giggs (4).
15 Use these to run (4).
18 Stadium or ground (5).
19 Muscle spasms caused through tiredness (5).
20 Running action (6).

DOWN

1 Chelsea's midfield anchorman Claude (8).
3 Cup games not decided during the first match (7).
4 County side from the Pride Park Stadium (5).
5 Found on the underside of football boots (5).
8 Made by a keeper (4).
11 If the midfield is not attacking enough, it is lying too _____ (4).
13 Parts of the ground that used to be all-standing areas (8).
14 Just got away, as from relegation (7).
16 Yorkshire club who play at Elland Road (5).
17 Selects for the team (5).

ACROSS

2 TV re-run, _____ replay (6).

6 Name of the original World Cup, the Jules _____ trophy (5).

7 A football should be shaped like this (5).

9 Number of teams in league play-offs (4).

10 Deep blue (4).

12 Competition to locate a football in a photo. _____ the ball (4).

15 David Beckham has Taurus as his _____ sign (4).

18 When you tire you are said to run out of this (5).

19 Game or activity like soccer, cricket or tennis (5).

20 Plymouth _____ (6).

DOWN

1 Scottish team from Pittodrie (8).

3 Welsh side from Ninian Park (7).

4 A reporter makes these when watching a game (5).

5 Coast to find Brighton and Portsmouth (5).

8 Leap off the ground (4).

11 Choose or elect a player of the year (4).

13 Team from Prenton Park (8).

14 Place to find City and Rovers (7).

16 Line of people waiting for tickets (5).

17 Favourite pre-match food of players in Italy (5).

No 20

ACROSS

2 North London side from Underhill Stadium (6).

6 Support for broken arm (5).

7 Reckless, dive-in tackle (5).

9 Former Liverpool star turned TV expert Hansen (4).

10 Bookable offence a _____ tackle (4).

12 Man Utd's legendary Irish winger George _____ (4).

15 Describes a goal scored all on your own (4).

18 A striker plays up _____ (5).

19 Tottenham striker Jermain (5).

20 Month when the football season starts (6).

DOWN

1 Side from the New Den (8).

3 Team managed by Arsene Wenger (7).

4 Wild cat from Hull? (5).

5 Legendary English keeper Gordon _____ (5).

8 Turnstile (4).

11 Had responsibility for a penalty (4).

13 Nickname of Bolton Wanderers (8).

14 Nickname for Everton (7).

16 Blackburn's Park (5).

17 Newspapers and TV (5).

No 21

ACROSS

2 Glasgow team with green and white hooped shirts (6).

6 Unfriendly opposition (5).

7 Spurs' Dutch midfielder _____ Davids (5).

9 1966 World Cup quote: 'Some people think it's all _____. It is now!' (4).

10 Owen and Ronaldo have been European Footballer of the _____ (4).

12 Rangers and Celtic are the 'Auld _____' (4).

15 If sent off you get an early _____ (4).

18 Raul plays for this country (5).

19 Skirmish on the pitch (5).

20 The best ever attained (6).

DOWN

1 Midland club, playing at the Ricoh Arena (8).

3 Club that Wayne Rooney left to join Man Utd (7).

4 Scottish river and a Scottish soccer side (5).

5 David Beckham started out on this wing (5).

8 Last but one round in a knock-out contest, _____ final (4).

11 Dutch side from Amsterdam (4).

13 Nickname for Grimsby sailors (8).

14 Team from the Deva Stadium (7).

16 Training gear _____ suit (5).

17 Bid for a player (5).

No 22

ACROSS

2 Obstruct, get in the way of (6).

6 Playing surface (5).

7 Team picture, _____ photo (5).

9 Describes a mammoth contest (4).

10 West Ham is from this end of London (4).

12 The letters F.C. stand for Football _____ (4).

15 Put your name on a contract and join a club (4).

18 Northern Ireland, Scotland, Wales and England are the teams from the British _____ (5).

19 England superstar Rooney (5).

20 Stages of a cup competition (6).

DOWN

1 Home of Bury (4,4).

3 Nickname of Newcastle (7).

4 Colchester and Southend are in this county (5).

5 Potteries side, _____ City (5).

8 Soccer team, _____WALL (4).

11 Part of leg protected by a pad (4).

13 Yorkshire team from Oakwell (8).

14 Liverpool's ground (7).

16 Nationality of Ryan Giggs (5).

17 Machine to cut the grass on a pitch (5).

No 23

ACROSS

2 Changing room place to wash (6).
6 Describes a terrible game (5).
7 Fulham play near the _____ Thames (5).
9 A rich chairman sometimes _____ a club (4).
10 Dismiss, as with a manager (4).
12 Expensive, like the fee for a top player (4).
15 Watch on TV (4).
18 Knock intentionally (5).
19 Games without definite results (5).
20 Lancashire club from Boundary Park (6).

DOWN

1 Fruity nickname of AFC Bournemouth (8).
3 Edinburgh side _____ _____ Midlothian (5,2).
4 Regulations, laws (5).
5 A sweeper aims to provide this for his defence (5).
8 Number of times a player can be shown the red card in a game (4).
11 The ref tosses this in the air before a match (4).
13 Man Utd's former skipper who moved to Celtic (3,5).
14 Welsh side known as The Swans (7).
16 Chelsea's Icelandic star Gudjohnsen (5).
17 BBC sports network _____ 5 Live (5).

ACROSS

2 Bids for a player (6).
6 Blackburn's Australian defender Lucas (5).
7 Closely contested (5).
9 ____ forward to take a penalty (4).
10 Day and time of fixture, or a fruit (4).
12 Team formation, four, ____ (4).
15 In short, soccer's world governing body (1,1,1,1).
18 Part of a soccer stadium, a ____ stand (5).
19 League chart (5).
20 Hand out penalty for foul play (6).

DOWN

1 Told off, spoken to by the ref (8).
3 Make-believe ____ football league (7).
4 Arsenal's Brazilian World Cup winner Gilberto (5).
5 Night-time illumination, flood____ (5).
8 Nil (4).
11 Threesome (4).
13 Lancashire team who play at Spotland (8).
14 Team from Ibrox (7).
16 Juventos and Lazio are clubs in this country (5).
17 Call by the ref to a player pretending to be injured (3,2).

No 25

ACROSS

2 The Glazer family became the ____ of Man Utd (6).
6 True fans are this (5).
7 A large pitch is said to have ____ of space (5).
9 Temporary transfer, on ____ (4).
10 Get a team place on merit (4).
12 A knock-out competition involving two stages, first and second ____ (4).
15 A referee must be this to both sides (4).
18 Loses footing (5).
19 Ready for action (5).
20 European international soccer side (6).

DOWN

1 Watford Road (8).
3 Midlands team from the Bescot Stadium (7).
4 Undersides of football boots (5).
5 Chelsea skipper John (5).
8 Speed (4).
11 Loud noise of the crowd (4).
13 Airborne bicycle kick (8).
14 Club associated with the legendary Tom Finney (7).
16 Item of football gear (5).
17 Winner! (5).

No 26

ACROSS

2 Nigeria and Ghana play in this continent (6).

6 Rich clubs can do this (5).

7 Jeer and mock rival fans (5).

9 Describes tidy play (4).

10 Kick off not on time (4).

12 Steal a last-minute goal (4).

15 Document for international travel (4).

18 Make your way up the league (5).

19 Tape of match action

20 A tidy player _____ and turns (6).

DOWN

1 The name of the game (8).

3 Ties up boot laces (7).

4 Injury time is _____ time (5).

5 Birmingham boss Steve (5).

8 Two boots make this (4).

11 Make someone fall (4).

13 Australian city and Leyton Orient's Road (8).

14 Teenager Theo signed by Arsenal from Southampton (7).

16 Losing semi-finalists meet to decide this place in the World Cup (5).

17 Clod of earth (5).

No 27

ACROSS

2 Attacker who plays out wide (6).

6 In going for a header you must not lead with this (5).

7 Box for the Queen at a soccer final (5).

9 Heads the ball down (4).

10 _____ Fife (4).

12 Don't get angry, keep cool and _____ (4).

15 Blackburn colours _____ and white (4).

18 Man Utd's Giuseppe _____ (5).

19 Paul Gascoigne's nickname (5).

20 Describes a thickset, well-built defender (6).

DOWN

1 Work out to keep fit (8).

3 International team managed by Steve Staunton (7).

4 Describes a noisy crowd (5).

5 Cash-starved club looks for a wealthy _____ (5).

8 Game plan (4).

11 Bottom of a boot (4).

13 Chelsea boss Jose (8).

14 Liverpool skipper Steven (7).

16 Liverpool's French forward Djibril (5).

17 Money paid to a player (5).

No 28

ACROSS

2 Physio's 'magic' piece of equipment (6).

6 A.E.T. stands for _____ Extra Time (5).

7 In pain, in _____ (5).

9 A passing team should play the ball to these (4).

10 Pulls on the opponent's shirt (4).

12 QPR home. Shepherd's _____ (4).

15 Costing nothing, a _____ transfer (4).

18 A playing surface should be flat like this (5).

19 A craze (5).

20 Scottish city with grounds at Tannadice Dens Park (6).

DOWN

1 Describes a shot that's not crooked (8).

3 End of season promotion decider (4,3).

4 Mistake (5).

5 Worn on the feet (5).

8 South American national soccer country, capital Lima (4).

11 Man Utd skipper _____ Neville (4).

13 London ground, White _____ _____ (4,4).

14 Take off a player and bring on another one (7).

16 County to find Exeter City (5).

17 Targeted (5).

No 29

ACROSS

2 Colour of Norwich City's strip (6).

6 Colour of Plymouth's strip (5).

7 Each player is presented with one after a Cup Final (5).

9 Place to buy souvenirs, the club _____ (4).

10 Complete the team. Roch _____ (4).

12 Penalty box, the penalty _____ (4).

15 Toy on a string or a word to describe a team going up and down divisions (4).

18 A keeper wants to keep a clean _____ (5).

19 The teams in the same section of a competition form this (5).

20 Name shared by Tranmere and Doncaster (6).

DOWN

1 Chelsea's Bridge (8).

3 Nationality of David Beckham (7).

4 Edges of the pitch (5).

5 Trickily change direction (5).

8 Trip to play different clubs (4).

11 Curved arc of a shot or header (4).

13 Blackburn centre-half, once of Bolton and Charlton (4,4).

14 Tottenham _____ (7).

16 _____ Alexandra (5).

17 Keen to do well (5).

No 30

ACROSS

2 Gaps, empty areas in the stand (6).

6 Cheer your head off, ____ the roof (5).

7 River that divides Forest and County in Nottingham (5).

9 Stay calm and keep this when the heat is on (4).

10 Manager Mr Curbishley (4).

12 Mesh on goalposts (4).

15 Something all clubs want! Another word for money (4).

18 Quick moving. The name of a bird (5).

19 Big occasion (5).

20 River connected with Liverpool (6).

DOWN

1 Mrs Beckham (8).

3 First name of the Glasgow team from Firhill Park (see 14 down) (7).

4 The defender should do this (5).

5 Scottish side ____ of the South (5).

8 Liverpool keeper Reina (4).

11 In two-legged contests these goals can count double (4).

13 A bad striker needs this kind of practice! (8).

14 Second name of 3 down and a prickly plant (7).

16 A cup, a trophy or anything there to be won (5).

17 Selecting a side of the world's best players is making a ____ team (5).

Answers

No 1

No 2

No 3

No 4

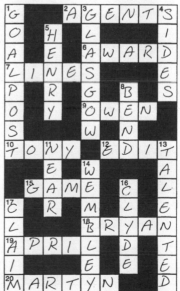

No 5

¹E			²U	N	I	T	E	³D
Q		⁵G	O					U
U		I	⁶R	O	M	A	N	N
⁷A	L	L	O	W				N
L		L	I			⁸F	E	
I		S	⁹C	A	R	D		
S		H	E			E		
¹⁰E	N	¹¹D	S		¹²Y	E	A	¹³R
		E	¹⁴S					E
	¹⁵P	A	R	K		¹⁶C		F
¹⁷L		L	I			A		E
O			¹⁸P	E	T	E	R	E
¹⁹S	H	A	R	P		C	H	E
E			E			H		E
²⁰R	O	B	E	R	T			S

No 6

¹T			²S	T	R	E	E	⁴T
U		⁵S	A					E
R		P	⁶C	R	O	W	D	D
⁷F	R	A	N	K				D
M		I	L			⁸I		Y
O		N	⁹E	N	D	S		
O		S				O		
¹⁰R	A	M	S		¹²C	L	A	¹³P
		O	¹⁴L					E
	¹⁵J	O	S	E		¹⁶C		D
¹⁷S		N	A			O		E
C			¹⁸D	I	V	E	R	E
¹⁹A	B	I	D	E		E		S
R			R			R		E
²⁰F	O	R	E	S	T			N

No 7

¹S			²T	³H	O	M	A	⁴S
E		⁵H	A					T
L		A	⁶T	U	G	A	Y	Y
⁷H	U	R	S	T				L
U		R	E		⁸C			E
R		Y	⁹R	A	I	D		
S			S		T			
¹⁰T	O	W	N		¹²E	Y	E	¹³S
		O	¹⁴R					I
	¹⁵R	O	S	E		¹⁶S		D
¹⁷C		D	F			P		E
O			¹⁸E	X	A	M	S	
¹⁹A	L	T	E	R		I		T
C			E			N		E
²⁰H	E	A	D	E	R			P

No 8

¹C			²A	³B	R	O	A	⁴D
U		⁵C		O				E
P		H	⁶O	R	D	E	R	E
⁷F	L	I	C	K				B
I		L	I			⁸K		Y
N		E	⁹N	I	N	E		
A		G				E		
¹⁰L	I	M	P		¹²H	E	L	¹³D
		A	¹⁴S					E
	¹⁵D	R	A	W		¹⁶D		F
¹⁷P		K	E			O		E
O			¹⁸E	D	W	I	N	E
¹⁹S	L	U	M	P		I		D
T			E			E		E
²⁰S	T	U	A	R	T			R

256

No 9

```
A  ·  B  R  A  Z  I  L
N  ·  S  A  ·  ·  ·  A
D  ·  P  N  I  C  K  Y
Y  O  U  N  G  ·  ·  E
C  ·  R  E  ·  N  ·  R
O  ·  S  R  Y  A  N  ·
L  ·  S  ·  M  ·  ·  ·
E  A  S  Y  ·  R  E  D
·  ·  C  ·  S  ·  ·  O
·  M  A  R  K  ·  H  U
J  ·  R  ·  Y  ·  A  T
A  ·  ·  B  E  N  C  H
M  E  D  A  L  ·  D  E
I  ·  ·  ·  U  ·  S  N
E  L  E  V  E  N  ·  D
```

No 10

```
P  ·  ·  G  R  A  H  A  M
L  ·  I  ·  E  ·  ·  ·  I
Y  ·  V  ·  S  K  I  L  L
M  O  O  R  E  ·  ·  ·  A
O  ·  R  R  ·  B  ·  ·  N
U  ·  Y  ·  V  A  L  E  ·
T  ·  ·  ·  E  ·  ·  U  ·
H  O  M  E  ·  B  E  A  T
·  ·  O  ·  S  ·  ·  ·  R
·  P  O  S  H  ·  D  ·  A
S  ·  D  ·  A  ·  A  ·  I
Q  ·  ·  ·  K  E  V  I  N
U  N  T  I  E  ·  I  ·  N
A  ·  ·  R  ·  ·  D  ·  N
D  A  N  I  S  H  ·  ·  G
```

No 11

```
W  ·  ·  D  I  R  E  C  T
E  ·  H  ·  P  ·  ·  ·  I
S  ·  A  ·  S  C  O  T  T
T  H  R  O  W  ·  ·  ·  L
B  ·  I  ·  I  ·  L  ·  E
R  ·  Y  ·  C  H  I  P  ·
O  ·  ·  ·  H  ·  V  ·  ·
M  I  K  E  ·  T  E  A  M
·  ·  I  ·  S  ·  ·  ·  O
·  S  C  O  T  ·  C  ·  L
P  ·  K  ·  E  ·  Y  ·  I
R  ·  ·  ·  W  I  G  A  N
E  X  T  R  A  ·  A  ·  E
S  ·  ·  ·  R  ·  ·  ·  U
S  P  E  E  D  Y  ·  ·  X
```

No 12

```
C  ·  ·  S  H  I  E  L  D
A  ·  P  ·  O  ·  ·  ·  A
N  ·  I  ·  R  O  B  I  N
A  S  T  O  N  ·  ·  ·  N
R  ·  C  ·  E  ·  P  ·  Y
I  ·  H  ·  T  R  A  P  ·
E  ·  S  ·  ·  ·  U  ·  ·
S  H  A  Y  ·  A  L  A  N
·  ·  W  ·  F  ·  ·  ·  I
·  S  A  M  I  ·  D  ·  G
F  ·  Y  ·  R  ·  U  ·  E
L  ·  ·  ·  P  E  T  E  R
A  L  L  O  A  ·  C  ·  I
G  ·  ·  ·  R  ·  H  ·  A
S  T  R  I  K  E  ·  ·  N
```

No 15

No 16

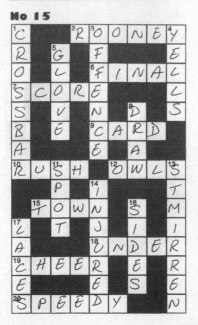

```
S  .  . S  C  O  R  E  R
E  .  G O  .  .  .  .  O
A  .  L R  I  V  A  L  L
G  R  E E  N  .  .  .  L
U  .  N E  .  V  .  .  S
L  .  N R  O  A  D  .  .
L  .  S O  .  S  .  .
S  A  F E  .  W  E  S  T
.  .  O .  B  .  .  .  R
.  H  U L  L  .  P  .  A
B  .  R O  .  A  .  N
A  .  . C  H  R  I  S
C  H  E C  K  .  I  .  F
K  .  . E  .  S  .  E
S  T  A N  D  S  .  R
```

```
M  .  . G  R  O  U  N  D
A  .  S E  .  .  .  .  E
K  .  T P  O  W  E  R  .
E  Q  U A  L  .  .  .  B
L  .  D A  .  S  .  Y
E  .  S Y  E  A  R  .
L  .  . S  .  .  U  .
E  N  D S  .  L  E  F  T
.  .  E .  E  .  .  R
.  L  E G  S  .  L  .  R
P  .  P C  .  E  .  A
I  .  . A  R  E  N  A
C  R  A M  P  .  D  .  C
K  .  . E  .  S  .  E
S  T  R I  D  E  .  S
```

```
A  .  A C  T  I  O  N
B  .  S A  .  .  .  O
E  .  O R  I  M  E  T
R  O  U N  D  .  .  E
D  .  T I  .  J  .  S
E  .  H F  O  U  R  .
E  .  . F  .  M  .  .
N  A  V Y  .  S  P  O  T
.  .  O .  B  .  .  R
.  S  T A  R  .  Q  A
P  .  E .  I  .  U  N
A  .  . S  T  E  A  M
S  P  O R  T  .  U  E
T  .  . T  .  O  E  R
A  R  G Y  L  E  .  E
```

```
M  .  B A  R  N  E  T
I  .  B R  .  .  .  I
L  .  A S  L  I  N  G
L  U  N G  E  .  .  E
W  .  K .  N  G  R
A  .  S A  L  A  N
L  .  . L  .  T  .  .
L  A  T E  .  B  E  S  T
.  .  O .  T  .  .  R
.  S  O L  O  .  E  O
M  .  K .  F  .  W  T
E  .  . F  R  O  N  T
D  E  F O  E  .  O  E
I  .  . E  .  D  .  R
A  U  G U  S  T  .  S
```

No 21
```
C . C E L T I C
O . R V . . . .
V . E N E M Y .
E D G A R . . .
N . H . T . S .
T . T . O V E R
R . N . M . . .
Y E A R . F I R M
. . J . C . . . A
. B A T H . T R I
O . X . E . R . O
F . S P A I N . .
F I G H T . C . E
E . . E . K . R .
R E C O R D . . S
```

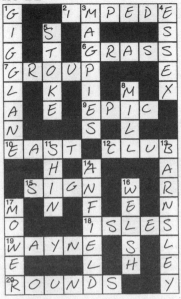

No 22
```
G . J U M P E D E
I . S A . . . S .
G T . G R A S S .
G R O U P . . E .
L K I . . . M X .
A E . E P I C . .
N S . . . L . . .
E A S T . C L U B
. H . A . . . . A
S I G N . . W R .
M . N . F . E . N
O . . I S L E S .
W A Y N E . S . L
E . . . L . H . E
R O U N D S . . Y
```

No 23
```
C . S H O W E R
H . C E . . . U
E . O A W F U L
R I V E R . . E
R . E T . O . S
I . R O W N S . C
E . . F . . C . .
S A C K . B E A R
. . O . S . . . O
. . V I E W . G Y
R . N . A . I . K
A . . N U D G E .
D R A W S . U . A
I . . . E . R . N
O L D H A M . . E
```

No 24
```
L . O F F E R S
E . L A . . . I
C . I N E I L L
T I G H T . . V
U . H A . Z . A
R . T Y . S T E P
E . . . . R . . .
D A T E . F O U R
. R . . R . . . O
. F I F A . I . C
G . O . N . T . H
E . . G R A N D .
T A B L E . L . A
U . . . R . Y . L
P U N I S H . . E
```

No 25

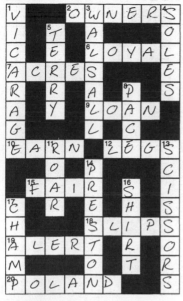

No 26

No 27

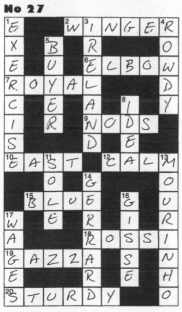

No 28

No 29

No 30

CAN WE HAVE OUR BALL BACK, PLEASE?

Football poems by Gareth Owen

A truly top-of-the-league collection of football poems!

Gareth Owen's lifelong love of football blazes through this stunning book of beautifully crafted poems. All the joy, sorrow and sheer fun of being a player and a fan can be found in this wonderfully funny and heartwarming collection.

Can We Have Our Ball Back, Please?

England gave football to the world
Who, now they've got the knack,
Play it better than we do
And won't let us have it back.